MW01096507

Empath Healing Workbook to Develop Your
Emotional Intelligence, Improve Self Esteem and
Self Confidence

(Self-protection, Emotional Healing, and Better
Relationships)

Jackson Miller

Published by Kevin Dennis

Jackson Miller

Empaths and Narcissistic Abuse: Empath Healing Workbook to Develop Your Emotional Intelligence, Improve Self Esteem and Self Confidence (Self-protection, Emotional Healing, and Better Relationships)

ISBN 978-1-989920-52-7

Legal & Disclaimer

The information contained in this book is not designed to replace or take the place of any form of medicine or professional medical advice. The information in this book has been provided for educational and entertainment purposes only.

The information contained in this book has been compiled from sources deemed reliable, and it is accurate to the best of the Author's knowledge; however, the Author cannot guarantee its accuracy and validity and cannot be held liable for any errors or omissions. Changes are periodically made to this book. You must consult your doctor or get professional medical advice before using any of the suggested remedies, techniques, or information in this book.

Upon using the information contained in this book, you agree to hold harmless the Author from and against any damages, costs, and expenses, including any legal fees potentially resulting from the application of any of the information provided by this guide. This disclaimer applies to any damages or injury caused by the use and application, whether directly or indirectly, of any advice or information presented, whether for breach of contract, tort, negligence, personal injury, criminal intent, or under any other cause of action.

You agree to accept all risks of using the information presented inside this book. You need to consult a professional medical practitioner in order to ensure you are both able and healthy enough to participate in this program.

Table of Contents

Introduction

Congratulations on downloading this book and thank you for doing so.

We may be communication every day, but the question is, are we *communicating well?* Oh yes, there certainly is a difference between the two. Great communication skills are the difference between a speaker who is just another individual who got up on stage and gave a speech and the speaker who left an impression so memorable that they had every member of the audience captivated from the moment they uttered their first word. Great communication skills are the difference between that coworker who gets along well and is able to perform excellently in a team and the one who struggles to make themselves understood.

Verbally or otherwise, if there's one thing you can be sure of, it is this.

Communication skills are an *asset.* You *need* them to flourish, you *need* them to thrive, you *need* them for success, and above all else, you *need* them to *survive.*

The art of effective communication was handed down from the ancient tradition known as *"Ars Oratoria"* that goes all the way back to ancient Greece. It has always been one of the main themes on human development and it focuses on one thing - the *importance of communication, AND how good communication can change your life for the better.*

No matter how good your leadership skills may be, or how brilliant your ideas are, everything that you're capable of means nothing if no one can see it. Why? Because they find it hard to *connect* to you. They find it hard to understand you, and you find it hard to express yourself. When you fail to relate and communicate, you fail to move one step forward towards your goal.

There are plenty of books on this subject on the market, thanks again for choosing this one! Every effort was made to ensure it is full of as much useful information as possible, please enjoy it!

Chapter 1: The Hsp Empath Defined

HSPs and Empaths are known for their high sensitivity. They are unlike everybody else because they can feel more.

Society largely misunderstands this sensitivity. Some consider it as weakness, especially since the culture nowadays is to be tough and ruthless. Others see it as a disorder. The things that bother an HSP or an Empath are easily ignored by the rest of the population; the common assumption is there must be something "wrong" with them.

Regardless of this, the sensitivity of HSPs and Empaths make them stand out in a good way. They naturally do things that others rarely or never do. Although they have their flaws, they can excel at their tasks if they set their minds and hearts to it.

The amazing thing about them is that they often have troubled lives, but that does not stop them from caring about others –

even if they are misunderstood or taken for granted. They do this because they can sense what others sense and feel what they feel. It is as if they are one with those around them.

Whether you are an HSP, or an Empath, or an HSP Empath, your sensitivity does not make you a weak person. It means that you are highly unusual with valuable gifts that must be used wisely.

What are the characteristics of HSPs?

Highly Sensitive Persons are those that are hypersensitive to stimuli (external and internal), have deeper cognitive processing, and high emotional reactivity. Their sensitivity is a result of the way their nervous system is constructed.

HSPs have higher sensitivity to the following internal and external stimuli:

Sensory stimuli (sight, sound, smell, taste, and touch)

Internal stimuli (pain, hunger, thirst, arousal, etc.)

Emotions (their own and others')

Subtle changes in other people and the surrounding
Their own intuitions

Chapter 2: Empaths And Energy Vampires

What are Energy Vampires? Energy vampires are those people who suck the energy out of you. Do you have relationships in your life where you feel like you give a lot and get nothing at all in return? Do you dislike conversations with a specific person because they always leave you feeling low, sad or even worthless? If you have answered yes to any of the above questions, then you probably have an energy vampire in your life. As the name already suggests, these are people who only 'take' from you, leaving you in an emotionally drained state. They cannot sustain a positive life-force on their own, and therefore, they latch onto others, feed off them, and eventually suck the life out of them!

Energy vampires come in various forms and they could be your friends, family, colleagues, clients, lovers, neighbors or even strangers. There are various behavioral categories of energy vampires, namely:

• *Fun haters* - They are incapable of just having fun and embracing joy. They will find ways to bring your mood down even in situations where you ought to be having the time of your life!

• *Bullies* - These are people who will stomp on 'smaller' guys in a bid to elevate their egos. Smaller does not necessarily mean physically but refers to people who are under them in social situations, in the family, or at work.

• *Jealous bees* - These are people who are unable to feel genuinely happy for anyone else, and as a result, they will trump on your successes.

• *Guilt trippers* - These kinds of energy vampires use shame to get exactly what they want. This means they will guilt trip you into all kinds of situations.

• *Blamers* - This kind will always blame everyone else for their issues, never taking any sort of responsibility for their actions.

- *Insecure ones* - These people have a lot of insecurities about themselves and they will strive to pull others down to their level of low self-esteem, whether consciously or not.

- *The whiners* - This refers to people who are always complaining about one thing or another, whatever the situation.

- *The gossipers and drama queens* - These are people who take pleasure in the failures of others and love dramatic situations.

- Others include the Debbie downers, the short-tempers, and so on.

If any of the people in your life fit this profile, then you most definitely have an energy vampire in your life. So the question is, how do you handle such people?

Dealing with Energy Vampires

Relationships are in essence an exchange of energy between two people. Therefore, whatever energy the other person is projecting, whether positive or negative, will eventually affect you directly since you are an empath! Positive vibes will mean you are surrounded by positivity and optimism. Energy vampires, on the other hand, will suck all the positive energy out of you, leaving you lifeless, pessimistic and hopeless.

The conversations we have on a daily basis have the ability to determine our emotions. Long conversations with an energy vampire may leave you feeling fearful, unloved, stupid, unworthy or even sick!

Handling energy vampires can get a bit tricky. As mentioned earlier, they could be people you love such as close family and friends. As an empath, your immediate reaction is to 'suck it up' and get along with everyone. However, this is at the expense of your sanity and progress. **The best way to handle energy-sucking relationships is to stop handling them!** This simply means cutting off people and relationships that are constantly weighing you down.

This is definitely not something that is easy to do. However, you must remember that as a guardian of your energetic space, it is your duty to surround yourself only with people who promote the same lifestyle as you, people who build you up as opposed to tearing you down.

In some cases, however, it may not be possible to completely cut them off. A good example would be if it is someone at your dream job, which obviously, you are not willing to let go of. In such instances, you can learn to cope by creating **energetic boundaries.** This means learning to separate your emotions from conversations with your energy vampires. This way you will be able to interact with them while also managing to keep your energy intact.

There are also some personal exercises to help you sustain your energy around an energy vampire. These are as follows:

Taking deep breaths and letting go. You have to make a conscious decision to not let their words or actions take up any space in you. Therefore, simply take deep breaths in such situations and 'delete'. Remember that you are in charge and no one can leech your energy if you do not give them permission to do so.

Keep things light by learning not to react on impulse. Instead, learn to be tactful, change the focus and bring the conversation back to a place where you once again feel comfortable. In situations where you feel belittled, re-affirm your self-worth! You deserve to only stay around people who inspire and build you to become the best.

Visualize an energy shield around you. This will help you to remain neutral such that their words or actions will in no way impact your life or actions!

All in all, remember that as an empath, you are highly susceptible to emotional abuse by an energy vampire. It is therefore up to you to make a conscious decision to shield yourself by simply determining the energy around you. Remember that you are who you surround yourself with!

Chapter 3: Empathic Psychic Abilities - Psychic Guide

What are Empathic Psychic Abilities?

An empathic psychic is also known as an "empath". Empaths have the ability to sense and experience the feelings of others, similar to the way telepaths can sense the thoughts of others. In fact, empathy and telepathy are closely related psychic abilities.

Usually, clairsentient psychics, (psychics with "clear feeling"), possess empathic psychic abilities. Empathic abilities are rare, but not unheard of.

Characteristics of an Empath

Empaths display these characteristics:

Extreme sensitivity to the feelings of others An acute awareness of their surroundings

Clear understanding of body language

Strong knowledge of human emotion The ability to feel deeper than others

The Empathic Spectrum

Not all psychics have the same amount of empathic power. Some psychics have only basic empathic abilities, while others have extremely advanced empathic powers. Most empaths fall somewhere in the middle.

Psychics with the most basic empathic abilities can sense what another is feeling, and can sometimes feel their emotions. These psychics can only understand some of what others are feeling.

Psychics with the most advanced empathic abilities can feel everything that other's are feeling. When engaged in empathic practice, these psychics often become so engaged people's feelings, that they momentarily loose sight of their own identity. Psychics such as these may be able to send emotional signals, and project their own feelings onto others.

Empathic Healing

Many empaths choose to use their abilities to heal others. Empaths usually place their hands on someone, in order to understand what they are feeling. This way, an empath can focus directly in on what the patient needs.

Powerful empathic psychics can share the feelings of others, in order to relieve their pain. Loss and grief are two common feelings that a powerful empath can share and lessen. To reverse this method, a psychic can also share their own feelings to spread joy and happiness.

A Gift or a Curse?

Because empaths spend so much time worrying about the feelings of others, they can forget to worry about themselves. Empaths may experience poor health as a result of self-neglect, emotional stress, and physical fatigue.

On the other hand, healing and spreading feelings of joy is a rare and wonderful gift! Hopefully you've learned something about empaths and empathic psychic abilities.

What does this mean?

If you think you might have empathic psychic abilities, you must develop your skills to uncover your true psychic power. Otherwise, your empathic power will never amount to anything useful! What a waste!

Chapter 4: Life Challenges

Here you will find some general tips for living your life as an empath.

Keep Focused
A hard thing to do, even if you're not an empath, is to evaluate your emotions. Especially if you're upset, depressed, or hurt. Negative emotions like these can cause you to become carried away. You won't think about them from the outside. When you notice that you are feeling a negative emotion, and nothing has happened to you to elicit this emotion, i.e. losing your keys, being cheated on, etc, you have to learn to step away from the negativity. Being able to move away from the negativity and look at it, instead of living it, you will be able to tell if it is your emotion or something you have picked up from somebody else. Again, you don't have to be in the same room with someone to pick up somebody else's

emotions. It is quite possible that you walked past someone in a crowd, or sat next to them in a theater, or just stood somewhere remotely near them at some point. Emotions, for an empath, can be contagious.

Shine Up Your Life

Now, I don't mean cleaning or shiny jewelry. I'm talking about crystals, gemstones, rocks, and minerals. A quick search on the internet will turn up a list of quite a few crystals that are perfect for empaths. Different crystals help with various things that help an empath to function such as, shielding, grounding, centering, emotional balance, and working through emotions. Some are able to give you an energy shield with contact. These come in handy when you are just learning to build your own shields, or if you have a lapse and forget to put up your shields when leaving the house. There are millions of ways of keeping the crystals close to you. Wearing them as jewelry is a great option. You can also carry them in your pocket, be mindful, though, some are fragile. Keeping them on your nightstand or near your computer at work, are also good options. If you don't wear jewelry, using them as a keychain is a great alternative. You can also hang them from your rearview mirror. Another option, that may seem strange, is to take them internally with a gemstone elixir. If you choose to take them internally, be sure the gem is safe to take internally. Some are not safe for consumption, while others are.

Learn to Breathe

Hopefully, you don't have to literally learn to breathe. Simple breath is an innate human ability for us to be able to live. For empaths, breath is a way to connect the body, mind, and spirit. Breath work is a great tool for empaths to have. According to Dr. Andrew Weil, the breath connects the unconscious and conscious mind. It can be used to control the involuntary nervous system. Breathwork has also been shown to decrease anxiety and increase spiritual awareness. It can also ground the mind, body, and spirit, and improve the communication pathways between mind and body. Empaths can use breathing to influence involuntary physical effects they feel when negative energies, such as anger, fear or sadness, pop up. Consciously changing the rhythms of your breath will calm the physical body and the emotional state of mind.

Panic will, unconsciously, cause people to take short, shallow gasps of air. This causes a lack of oxygen, which will restrict blood flow, and cause muscles to tense. An effective, proven, way to reduce tension, feel relaxed, and reduce stress, is to take full, deep breaths. Systems such as yoga, T'ai chi, and Pranayama offer ways to use your breath in a direct way to enhance your body's energy and help to relieve old emotions. According to Stanislav Grof holotropic breathwork allows people to transcend the narrow boundaries of our body and reclaim our identity. With the controlled breathing, our natural inner wisdom uses the opportunity to work towards mental, emotion, spiritual, and physical healing. The resources to find breathwork information is abundant. You can find Dr. Andrew Weil's 4-7-8 breathing technique on YouTube. He also has audio books on breathwork.

Alternate nostril breathing, also known as nadi shodhana, is a great way to balance your inner masculine and feminine energy. This is a simple practice. Sit in a comfortable place with your back straight and eyes closed. Place your right thumb on the edge of your right nostril and your right ring finger hovers over your left nostril. First, close off the right nostril with your thumb and inhale through the left for a 3 count. Now lift your thumb and close the left nostril with your ring finger, and exhale through your right nostril for a 3 count. Then breathe in through your right nostril for a 3 count. Close your right nostril and exhale through the left for 3 counts. That was a single round. When you first start practicing do just 9 rounds and slowly work your way up to 20. If you need to see how to do this you can find a lot of videos on YouTube. You may get a little dizzy the first time you practice this. If you do stop and breathe normally until the dizziness passes.

Large Groups
If at all possible, avoid large crowds. Social anxiety is a problem that empaths have to face. Sometimes without knowing why. Many may be written off as shy. It can even negatively impact friendships because the empath is afraid to go out when they know a large crowd is inevitable. Each individual emotion may not be felt, but being surround by a crowd of people, with varying degrees of emotion, can make it feel like you are being crushed by a brick wall. This doesn't have to interfere with your social life. You can still go out to the movies or clubs with

friends. And you will eventually have to go to the grocery store, but be aware of these problems. That way you can plan for future outings. When you know you need groceries, go to the store on weeknights when they aren't as typically packed. If you plan on going to the movies go at a time where they won't be as packed, and make sure you sit next to a friend that you can focus on. Having an aisle seat may also help. Eating a healthy, high protein, meal beforehand will help you to stay grounded during the outing.

Let It Out

Bottling up emotions can be detrimental to people without the ability of empathy. It has been known to cause health problems, even heart attacks. When something is bottled for too long, eventually it will explode. Take a bottle of soda. Most everybody knows the experiment of dropping a mentos into a bottle of coke. You drop mentos into the bottle of soda and quickly screw the cap back on. As the mentos mixes with the soda, the soda begins to foam and the pressure begins to build in the bottle. Eventually, the top explodes and soda bursts out. The bottling of emotions works much in the same way. When the top explodes you may end up saying things that you'll regret later. You may possibly hurt somebody. It could also lead to an implosion, where you end up hurting yourself more. You can become emotionally crippled. It can end up damaging your aura, cause mental instability, clog your chakras, and cause you to become physically ill. A great way to deal with your emotions is to let them out. You can express them by talking to a close friend, or, if you don't want to talk to somebody, you could journal, paint, draw, and write, whatever that speaks to you.

Keep a Good Outlook
"All the suffering in the world arises from wanting happiness for the self. All the

happiness in the world comes from wanting happiness for others," Shatideva.

If you have your shields down you may end up feeling the sorrows of the entire world. A Unicef commercial could come on TV and trigger it. Before you have time to realize what's going on you start crying uncontrollably. They may end up making you feel guilty that you aren't able to help all of the children in the entire world from hunger and poverty. It could also be one of the several commercials about abused and starving animals that could send you over the edge. It's hard to look at innocent children and animals, and know you can't help them all. You could do charity work, and donate to foundations, but in the end, you see these commercials, or news articles, and feel like you're not doing enough. This overwhelming sense that you could be doing more might come up at any moment. An innocent comment made by a friend could cause it. You can't let this control you. Remind yourself that the wealthiest person in the world couldn't rescue all the animals or help all the children. You're not the richest person in the world, you're you, and you are doing the best you can. Whatever you do to help, will be felt on a global level. It may not seem like much to you, but think of how the animal you helped feels, or the child, or the homeless person. Remember these quotes when you feel like you need to do more: "The smallest act of kindness is worth more than the grandest intention," Oscar Wilde, and "We can't help everyone, but everyone can help someone," Dr. Loretta Scott.

You can adopt and change the life of a child, or dog, or cat. Small changes really are able to make a big difference for at least one person. If you want to help on a global scale there are millions of charities that you can give to that provides water, chickens, and cows to villages in Haiti and Africa. You can donate to websites such as http://www.aidforafrica.org/donate/, which provides necessities to families and children in sub-Saharan Africa. You can also donate to sites like https://www.booksforafrica.org/donate.html that help to provide children with books for education. On a smaller scale, you could spend your free time helping local charities and organizations. You can help out at rescue missions, soup kitchens, or animal shelters. Although, if you're like me, an animal shelter may not be the smartest choice because you may end up with a houseful of pets. You could also become a Big Brother or Big Sister. If you're new to donation, or you're not sure about a charity, be sure to check them out on Charity Watch before donating. A word of advice, I wouldn't donate a book in honor of a friend or family member for Christmas unless they like that sort of thing. They may be upset if you don't get them an actual gift.

There Are Others

The internet comes in handy for empaths. It's an easy way for you to find and connect with other people that have similar abilities and issues. If you've had to go at this alone, not understanding what an empath is, and handling the crazy flow of emotions, you might have thought at one point you might be crazy. With all the good things you can find on the internet to help you, there is probably an equal amount of bad things. WebMD is probably the biggest. It causes problems for people that are able to think rationally, but for an empath, it can be a death sentence. You look up a few simple symptoms, and you find out you have an incurable disease. It always seems like they list the worst ailments at the top of the list, so my advice would be for you to steer clear of WebMD. Instead of turning to medically based websites, turn to communities of empaths, and like-minded people. You can find them in forums, Facebook groups, and many other places online. A good place to go is meetup.com. All you have to do is sign up, put in your zip code, and do a quick search, and you will be presented with local places and people to meet with so you don't feel so alone. A common symptom of empaths is feeling alone. They can't truthfully and openly talk to anybody because they will end up thinking they are crazy. Finding locations of local new age shops will give you a multitude of people that won't look at you as if you have three heads. You may even find other empaths. Remember that you are never alone. Once you start learning the shielding and grounding techniques coming up, and find friends who understand you, you won't have to live in solitude anymore. Have faith, it is possible to control this.

News

Avoid media at all costs. Depending on how long you have been working with your ability, your strength, and the weakness of your shields, you may be vulnerable to news stories. Whenever a tragedy hits near you or in the world, avoiding the TV and internet news would be your best bet. Seeing the people involved could cause an emotional connection with them, causing you distress. The news works on sharing stories of extremely emotionally charged stories. Unfortunately, most of those emotions are negative. Positive news stories don't make for good ratings. This makes the news a mine field of emotions for empaths. It may seem that you are out of the loop, but you could set up an app on your phone to give you little blurbs about what's going on. That will keep you from getting the full story, and once you read the blurb you can decide if you think it's safe enough for you to read. Only you know how strong and susceptible you are to emotions.

Melodies
Music can have a huge impact on empaths. Just like the news, they can cause different emotions. Some songs make you happy, while others can cause you to cry for hours on end. Recently I went to a performance about the life of a Native American hero. Before the show

began one of the actors came out and played a few songs on a courting flute. It was all I could do to keep from blubbering and freaking out the woman sitting beside me. The heightened sensitivity helps empaths to use music for healing. Try soothing instrumental music. Mantra music is also a great choice. My go to is the spa channel on Pandora.

"Music takes us out of the actual and whispers to us dim secrets that startle our wonder as to who we are, and for what, whence, and whereto," Ralph Waldo Emerson.

Food

Health and food are an important part of everyday life for anybody, but health plays an even bigger part in an empath. Emotional energy can have a large impact on your physical health. An empath's body takes constant hits from stress and energy. As mentioned earlier, this includes the weight you gain to help insulate yourself from negativity. Having good physical health gives an empath a good, strong foundation. A good diet includes colorful, bright, rainbow of veggies. Raw or lightly cooked, and not drowned in starchy sauces, are best. Fish is a great meat, with minimal amounts of red meat. You don't have to vegetarian or vegan to be healthy. Meat is fine, just be mindful of the type and how much you consume on a weekly basis. A biggie is to drink lots and lots of water. Cutting down on processed foods such as sugar and corn syrup are also great. Also cut back on foods that contain chemicals, like diet sodas, and caffeine. I'm not telling you not to eat any of this; I'm just saying make sure your body really wants it. Everything is fine in moderation. Just don't make a habit of eating bad, junky foods.

Movement
Exercise is an important part of any health regimen. Many people think that exercise has to be hard. There's no need for it to be at a gym, with a trainer, or running until

you throw up. You don't have to have six-pack abs or be able to bench press 300 pounds. This is just about keeping you healthy and toned. This will provide you with a strong base so that you can control our emotions, handle the emotions you receive from others, and work with energy. Your spirit, mind, and body is your foundation, and it needs to be kept in balance. Your exercise can be anything that you want. Any sort of movement that gets your heart pumping and blood flowing, something that leaves you feeling good. It could be dancing, yoga, pilates, swimming, running, or just walking around your community. It's sometimes hard to figure out what you want to do. Many think they have to do what everybody else does, but you don't. Find something that you enjoy doing, that's the key. If you enjoy doing it, then you will continue to do it. If you like dancing, Zumba is a great option, that's what I enjoy doing. There is something out there for you, you just have to find it.

Vitamins

Healthy diet and exercise are the top two most important parts of good physical health, but vitamins play an important role as well.

A lot of people like to say that if you eat the right foods you are receiving all the vitamins that you need. That's not necessarily true. Some people aren't able to eat foods that contain certain vitamins and minerals because they are allergic to the food. It's also proven that our soil isn't as nutrient rich as it use to be 50 years ago, so the food doesn't contain as many vitamins. It may seem like a hassle trying to remember to take a bunch of pills every morning, but think of why you're doing it. It's good for you. If you're not sure what you need to take you could see a holistic doctor that can steer you in the right direction. There are also some online stores that offer a quiz that can give you a rough estimate of what you need. Just be cautious about quizzes. A family health care provider may be your first thought, but they aren't really in the vitamin industry. In my personal opinion, the holistic doctor is the best course of action until you get used to telling what you need.

Apple Cider Vinegar is something a lot of health-conscious people will tell you to use. It's important to get Apple Cider Vinegar with "mother". Besides the fact that the bottle will say "with mother", it will have cloudy residue on the bottom of the bottle, and you have to shake it before use. The most popular brand is Bragg's Apple Cider Vinegar, but other brands have started carrying ACV with mother. Two teaspoons are all you need to take each morning. You could choose to take them as a shot with some water or fruit juice, or you could make a cup of tea. I personally take a cup of water, a couple of teaspoons of lemon, and then two teaspoons of ACV, heat it up and have it before my morning cup of coffee. You can also add some honey to help with the tartness of the vinegar. Do what works best for you. There is a myriad of reasons to use ACV. One of the main reasons is that it raises your body's ph level. This helps to keep bugs, mainly mosquitoes, away. Mosquitoes like you sweet, not tart.

Neighborhood Counselor

At some point, your friends, family and complete strangers will tell you their problems. When strangers talk to you this could be in the line at a coffee shop, or on a park bench. This will eventually end, and you probably won't ever see them again. Friends and family, on the other hand, may take advantage of you. They might see you as their own, 24 hours, 7 days a week, therapist. Empaths will want to help. They don't want to tell somebody in need no, but when friends and family come to talk, empaths will open and take in all the negative emotions. This is draining to the whole body, and when it is constantly happening you will likely stay in a constant state of depletion. You can only help so much, and if you don't keep yourself healthy then there will be nobody there for them to turn to. You have to put your own well being first. You will have to figure out nice ways to end conversations when you've had enough. You have to set some sort of limit especially if you have to deal with somebody that never actually wants to take your advice. They just want spew out their problems without learning how to fix them. Sometimes you just need to use your own compassion on yourself.

Keep Your Shields Up

An empath without proper training and practice, and without shields or grounding knowledge is like a fresh wound. You will be driven crazy by the attack of all the senses around you. Then you will end up absorbing all these emotions into you. This can lead to emotional problems or even physical ailments. The process of shielding is learning how to build a wall around your aura so other people's problems and emotions will just deflect off, instead of you absorbing them. It's not hard once you learn how to, but it has to be constantly practiced until you're able to do it without thought. Grounding is much like a grounding wire in electrical wiring. It allows you to be able to take in the emotions of others and allow it to pass through you to the ground to be cleansed. This is extremely important if you plan on being involved in healing or touching. You should never hold onto the negativity that you pull from others, it will cause major problems for you.

Weeding Through Your Friends

Empaths seem to have the ability to attract certain types of people; psychic, energy, or emotional vampires. You'll know when you've encountered this type of person because you will feel drained after just five minutes of talking to them. I have a family member that does this to me. I can be around her for a few minutes and I start to get a migraine. They may just complain and drone on and on. Others may be charming and friendly, those are sometimes harder to spot. No matter which one they are they are either consciously or subconsciously attaching themselves to you, draining you. After they're gone, they have received a boost from chatting with you, but it leaves you feeling like you've run a marathon. You need to cut down on the time spent with these friends, if not cut them out completely. It may seem mean and hard to do, but it's for your own good. It's not healthy to be in a relationship like that, and there's no need to add to your daily minefield you tip toe through. You may have known them for a long time, you still need to re-evaluate the balance of the relationship.

Celebrate

You are unique. You have a path, and some people are not as fortunate. You walk this earth to help and heal people that need you. This could be small things, where you soothe people's emotions that you come in contact with, or on a bigger scale working as a healer in a medical center. It doesn't matter what your career is, whether you work in a healing occupation, or as a teacher, or sales associate, you can and will impact people in small ways that grow to make a big difference. Don't be afraid of your ability, or think of it as a curse. Trying to deny or ignore what you are can cause an imbalance. This will end up causing physical side effects or stay bottled until it eventually explodes.

Have Some R&R

Empaths require frequent amounts of quiet time to recharge. Even if you're experienced and you can shield automatically, it still takes work and will drain you. To people on the outside energy healing will look like you're doing nothing, but it still drains your body and mind. Everybody has some level of responsibilities, whether you're married with children or single, you need to take at least a few minutes every day to be by yourself. This could be some breathing work, meditation, or snuggle time with your pet. Snuggling with a pet, or going outside for a few minutes will give you an extra boost. If you live in a big city like New York or Chicago, a good thing for you might be to try to get away to a more earthy setting at least twice a year. That might mean just heading to the beach, or finding a mountain retreat. Nature will help to recharge you and balance you out. Another great practice to have is earthing. Earthing is having direct skin to earth contact. This could mean just walking around outside barefoot in grass or dirt. You could also hug a tree, or take a dip in a local river or stream. It's important to keep a close connection with the earth.

Schedules

Empaths will often want to keep a steady routine, it's a comforting normalcy in an otherwise crazy day. This can cause burnout, which may lead to you spending all night reading a book when you should be sleeping. Being aware of this can help to prevent this from happening. If you like to keep a schedule, then make sure you block off some time for fun things you like to do. Block off a few hours a day for reading, or video games, or for some relaxation time. With cell phones, we have unlimited amounts of reminders at our fingertips. Set reminders on your phone for important things you need to remember to do.

Add Some Salt

I'm not talking about upping your sodium intake. Sea salt is the best energy purifier out there. It is able to dissolve negative energies. It's also a great tool for cleansing your crystals. Crystals have to be cleansed otherwise they hold onto all the energies that they have been in contact with and rub off on you. By soaking them in sea salt overnight, they will be purified and released of all those energies. You can buy sea salt lamps that help purify the energy in your house. Another way to use sea salt is to take a bath in it. It will help to release negative energies from your body. There is no need to buy the super expensive stuff at a fancy store either. Non-iodized sea salt from your local grocery store works just as well. Sea salt has become a big seller in the bath and body departments. You can find shampoo, body scrubs, bath bombs, and shower gels. You can also make your own, which is my preference. For a simple salt scrub recipe, just add olive oil to a cup of salt. Add a little bit at a time until the salt starts to look wet. For a reference, it should resemble grits.

No Means No

Empaths want to help everybody, and will sometimes say yes to a request without thinking of the consequences. It's very easy for an empath to get attached to being the nice person. Feeling all the negative emotions may not be fun, but trying to heal all of them isn't going to serve you or the other person. You might agree to do something that you don't have the time or resources to do. Whether the person's emotions are super strong and needy, or they quietly creep in you and trick you into thinking they're your own, you may find it hard to say no. After you finished helping them is when you realize what you've done. It could have caused you to miss an important meeting at work, or it's three in the morning and now you'll only get four hours of sleep. Empaths don't want to seem selfish, it's not in their nature. Yet you still need to look out for yourself. Make sure before you say yes that their problem is worth your help, and how much energy will need to be devoted. It is good to be compassionate, but without going beyond your limits. You never go beyond that line. For an empath, that line may be a little fuzzy. Once you are able to tell where that line is it will make your relationships clearer. It's not healthy to try to protect others from their emotions. It will keep them from being able to grow up. Learn how to say no. There's no need to be rude, but you don't need to give into everybody's needs.

Catch Some Z's

Sleep is important for anybody's health and wellbeing, but for an empath, it's paramount. Empaths have an added level of stress that other people don't and won't understand. Six to eight hours of sleep at night is the recommended amount for adults. Try to get a full night's sleep as often as possible. If you have problems with insomnia an over the counter option is melatonin. Melatonin is the hormone our body lets off at night that helps us get to sleep. It is also the only hormone that you can buy in the vitamin section at your grocery store. You can also try relaxation methods such as tea, binaural beats or hypnosis music, meditation, breathwork, anything that relaxes you to sleep. If at all possible try not to turn to prescriptions drugs to help with sleep. You might sleep all through the night, but the quality of sleep probably won't be as good, and the synthetic drug isn't good on your body. Also, don't drink alcohol before bed. Alcohol may seem to put you to sleep, but you will end up waking in the middle of the night when it wears off. Having a regular good night's sleep will help you to maintain the ability to automatically ground and shield, which, as you've learned, is very important for an empath to function.

H2O

Water has therapeutic properties for an empath. Just the sound of running water can be soothing. Natural clean running water, such as a stream, is able to boost positive energy levels. It's great for an empath to live near water, but that's not always possible, so visiting a natural water source regularly is a good alternative. To receive healing benefits of water it needs to running, so setting out a bowl of still water isn't going to give you the same results. There are lots of options to bring running water into your house so that you can reap the benefits. You can easily buy a little table top fountain online. I'm sure there is probably a way to learn to make your own if you prefer to go that route. If neither one of those options works for you, just make sure to take lots of showers and sea salt baths.

Develop Your Chakras
Your chakras play an important part in your life as an empath. Most of the times empaths know what they should do or say, and how to make good on keeping boundaries, but they have trouble actually following through. The throat chakra needs to be opened. The throat chakra is the center of being able to express personal truth. When you open your throat chakra you will be able to express your true needs and feelings. Some exercises for opening the throat chakra are; singing, sharing feelings with friends and meditating on the throat chakra. Crystals for the throat chakra are; turquoise, amazonite, and blue lace agate. These would be good crystals to wear as a necklace so that they will be in contact with the throat chakra.

Another chakra that may need to be developed for an empath is the root chakra. The root chakra helps an empath to deal with being in the world. When it is open you are grounded and present for whatever is going to happen. A closed root chakra can cause you to be dissociative, fearful, and have difficulty staying present. Opening the root chakra helps to release fears that keep you from your highest manifestation. Exercises that help to open the root chakra is imagining you are sending roots into the earth from your feet. Imagine that you breathe from your roots. When you inhale, breath in energy from the earth. When you exhale, release anything that doesn't serve you. Crystals for the root chakra are; obsidian, hematite, and red jasper.

Chapter 5: The Untrained Empath

What Is An Untrained Empath?

Empaths who are unconscious of their abilities or do not know how to use them properly are known as untrained Empaths. Untrained Empaths often absorb the problems of the world along with other people's problems. When an untrained Empath tunes into the physical, mental, and emotional pain of others, they often identify the pain to be their own and shut down or have a meltdown.

Untrained Empaths can intensely feel what others feel, but do not have control of how it affects themselves. For instance, an untrained Empath might see someone sitting alone on a park bench and feel their sadness within them. They would then mistake the other person's sadness for their own and begin to feel confused as to why their mood switched all of the sudden. This can be very overwhelming and create a great deal of turbulence in day to day life.

When you are an Empath without knowing so, things like this can be a very challenging to overcome. Many untrained Empaths are led to believe that something is wrong with themselves and they begin to seek medical help. Unfortunately, the medical industry has not yet learned how to deal with highly sensitive people and has no idea what to do. Often times doctors or psychiatrists subscribe medication or treatments that are destructive to the overall health and wellness of the Empath. This can result in the numbing of the Empaths sensitivity, but not a resolution.

Untrained Empaths are often led to believe that they are crazy or neurotic, and that their heightened sensitivity is just an unstable personality trait. They are convinced that they are bipolar or that they themselves are experiencing all of the emotional flux, when it is usually the emotions and pains of others. This can be extremely misguiding and can lead to different alleys of confusion and self destruction. If you are experiencing this, it is important to seek alternative paths that help, and take action accordingly to a method that work for you.

How Can I Train Myself?

Firstly, recognize that you are highly sensitive. Take a deep breath... now begin to accept yourself 100%. Training may take a bit of time and maybe a breakdown or two, but none of it can truly help until you learn to love yourself unconditionally.

Secondly, start to study yourself thoroughly. Begin noting things that trigger you, and learn about your own unique sensitivity. Surround yourself with people who are willing to help you and who accept you. Above all, understand that you are a beautiful creation of the universe and you are strong.

Lastly love yourself☐

Chapter 6: Using Emotional Quotient To

Your Advantage

What is emotional quotient?

You've probably heard of IQ (measure cognitive abilities) and not EQ. Emotional quotient is sometimes referred to as Emotional intelligence. But you might be wondering what it means. Well, this is the level of measure of personal emotional intelligence.

Also, it's the ability of a person to know their emotions and those of others and differentiate the variety of emotions correctly. Emotional quotient is useful in our day to day activities; with it, you will be able to guide your behaviors and influence that of others. After all, you can give others the power that you only possess.

Additionally, this is a vital factor in all aspects of your life. That is your mental, spiritual, and social life. It helps you connect at a deeper self. And mold you into a desirable human being. EQ is what enables have to have serious conversations with your partner or empathize with your friend when they are going through a challenging situation or discipline your children when they do wrong.

EQ assists in emotional and social learning in children. College students with EQ get to perform better engage in more social interactions and develop constructive behaviors rather than the destructive.

Components of emotional quotient
Self-regulation- You need to recognize yourself and your behaviors. Then, you regulate, express and manage your emotions
Self- awareness- self-awareness acts as a foundation EQ .understanding your

feelings is vital as tend to extend those emotions to others

Social skills – social skills helps to foster interaction amongst people. Those with high EQ, can interact well with others and expressing themselves is never a hard task

Empathy- empathy enables you to register people feelings, known how they feel

Motivation- people with high emotion quotient are self-motivated. They are happy achieving internal success, rather than external. They work hard towards their goals. Achievements such as wealth, respect, or fame don't fascinate them much. But reaching their goals is what entices them.

Characteristics of people with high EQ

They have a healthy work-life balance- they know how to interact with people at workplaces and air out their views when they don't agree with issues.

Easy going- you can talk to them, with feeling intimidated

They are grateful- they don't take their lives for granted, and little things fascinate them. They are thankful for everything life family, life, and also their jobs.

open-minded- they are not confined to their beliefs of a certain thing, but are open to new ideas and are ready to embrace them

They know their strengths are always willing to work on their weaknesses.

Forgive others easily- they don't hold grudges but forgive others

Know them- they know their likes, dislikes, and what they stand for in life.

Empathetic- they put themselves in people's shoes and can sympathize with them.

Those without emotional quotient

People are different, and forcing other people to behave in a certain way can end up bad. You don't force someone to become what you want, but you let them willingly become. EQ is not necessarily inherited but is a skill that can be developed over some time if you train.

The following are characteristics of people without EQ;

Unable to control their emotions. Can react veraciously to anger situations.

They don't care about o0her people's feelings. Or instead, they are clueless. They don't notice if someone is sad or happy.

They don't know how to deal with sadness or grief. In short, emotional scenes in movies don't move them. You neither cry and feel the part

Importance of developing emotional quotient

When you develop this skill you get to;

Improve your relationships. It could be with your partner's friends, neighbors, or relatives. You build on your communication skills and know-how to persuade, being open, and channel your emotions.

Understand yourself and others well- you don't forever become clueless, but you can study how you react to your emotions and also you know how others in your environment

You connect with others. Most human beings crave connection. You connect with others at a deeper level. When you connect with others; you boost your overall performance in school, home, and also work.

Skills that will assist you in developing emotional quotient

Channel your emotions well

Are you the type to break things when angry? Recognize how you react to situations. Anger can be destructive, and you should learn how to control it. Share the joyful moments with the people around you.

Learn how to motivate yourself

Appreciate yourself in everything g you do. Believe you can do anything and you will. Do something even you don't feel like doing. It could be waking up, writing, etc. self- motivation pushes you to be a better you.

Practice self- awareness

Know yourself. Investigate yourself and learn the little aspects you didn't S know about yourself. What you feel. Remove distractions from your life and learn how to motivate yourself.

Recognize the way other people feel. Understand people and listen to people more. People are vulnerable. When you recognize other people's feelings, you will be able to foster a romantic atmosphere, also respect other people's needs and wants. You become selfless.

Self-awareness techniques

Self-awareness means that you can recognize yourself on a personal level. This is s inclusive of your strengths weaknesses, emotions, thoughts, and also believes. Self-awareness makes you understand people and return their feelings,

Also, you can correct your behaviors and improve yourself for the better things about you start to change, and you become more optimistic when it comes to life. Self-awareness increases your level of EQ and gives you a sense of direction in your future. Lastly, you learn how to optimize yourself.

The following are self-awareness techniques:

Have a journal
In this journal scribble everything and anything that goes on in your life. Your, goals, your, strengths, your weakness, your success stories, among other things, a journal helps you free yourself from

various emotions, especially those of anger. You vent out and in return, become happier.
You learn to appreciate yourself more and work hard towards achieving your goals
Be objective about yourself.

Self-awareness enable3 you learn and accept yourself the way you are. You learn more things about yourself. What perceptions do you have when you experience certain aspects of life?
Learn how you react to happy situations, sad situations, or people. Write things you are proud of and what makes you. Being objective enables you to encourage others to be the better versions of them, as you are.

Meditate
Meditation is a good, mindfulness activity. It helps you relax your mind. This is a high daily activity of self-awareness.
Find a quiet, comfortable place to start your meditation. Then, close your eyes

and be in the moment and, lastly breathe. Meditation helps you relax. You reflect on yourself, your goals, and assist you to focus more.

Ask feedback from your friends.
Feedback is important. Ask your friends for honest feedback. They should tell you how you behave and how they perceive you. They act as a mirror. Honest feedback will enable you to know yourself more and also know the qualities to improve.

Interrogate yourself.
Ask yourself questions concerning a different aspect of your life.
They could be your likes, dislikes, what you are good at, things that make you happy or the one that interests, write down on your journal. You can always review later.

Take personality tests
Several personality tests are online. With them, you are enabled to measure your innate capabilities as a human being. The

test gives you a good self-awareness ground, and you can improve. Personality tests don't need to be 100%.

Finally, Self-awareness is crucial as it helps you become the best version of yourself.

Self -management

Self-management means taking responsibilities and the actions that you take in life. You become the boss of you and regulate your behaviors, emotions, thoughts, in different situations.

The following are rules of self-management rules. They are what guide you in your self-management journey:

Cultivate trust- you need to created trust or be trustworthy so that people will have faith in you.

Be yourself - don't copy others. You are amazing the way that you are. Copying others will stop you from living your best life. Be original

Have a courtesy -courteous phrases like thank you, sorry, and excuse me don't cost any dime. They make you responsible, and a respected person as you mind what others feel.

Always learn to say no- you don't have to say yes, to all situations. Saying no to friends outing is okay as it can give you more time for yourself.

Speak up- don't be quiet when things are wrong; people need to know you and what you stand for. You don't expect people to hear what is in your heart or mind, dear.

Keep your promises. When you promise a thing to someone strive to fulfill it. Keeping promises enhances the trust that people have in you

Take care of yourself- If you don't, then who will? Make yourself the priority. Exercise, meditate, ad eats healthily and have fun in all things that fascinate you.

Key self-management skills

The following skills will help you manage your skills.

Initiative

From the name, this means that you take actions concerning different events that take place in your life. You don't need one to tell you that something needs to be done but, instead you, do it. You are not pushed but you self-motivate yourself.

Organization

With organization skills that plan what you need from most relevant to the least important. The organization ensures you get most done out of your daily activities.

Accountability

Accountability means that you are responsible for yourself. When things go wrong, you can rectify without blaming others. Blaming sucks and it's only for those who don't want to own up to their mistakes. Accountability enables you to improve your skills.

Importance of self- management

Self- management enables you to take advantage of rare opportunities.

When called upon to take on duty, you don't hesitate since you know how to organize yourself and are ready to grasp any opportunities that present themselves.

Focus on your goals-

For goals to achieved, several things need to take place. That is lots of work hard and commitment. But, self-management becomes your drive to do anything.

Become comfortable when working and know how to organize time

The saying goes to say that time is money. When you know how to plan your time, then you get a lot done in your life. You become happier as your productivity rates improve. When working, you don't have any worries because you know yourself more.

Control your emotions

Knowing how to deal with situations and finally you know to behave. Getting along with others won't be difficult, as you have empathetic s skills in you. You know what you want and exactly what you stand for.

Social awareness
Social awareness is the understanding of one's environment or community. That could be the culture, norms and regulations, and problems. You understand your environmental well and discover how to deal with the conditions surrounding it. Also, you can interact with people and know how they feel. With this, you can deal with intrapersonal and societal problems.

With this, you can solve personal problems. In this technological world, Social media and video conferencing is not a big deal. But in reality, people crave attention. Technology has resulted in social isolation.

Importance of social awareness

When you lack social awareness, then, you will be a misfit to society. You need to understand what is going on around your environment. The advantages include:

It helps to understand and communicate with people. Speaking to people is important. When you as aware of what is going around you, then you will be able to conduct a conversation.

You become more empathetic- social awareness enables you to notice pain in people. Hence, you help others deal with their grief.

You develop problem-solving skills- when a problem arises, then you can come up with a solution and solve it.

You get respect from people- people begin respecting you as they feel you understand them and can solve certain situations.

How to develop social -awareness skills
Become self-aware

When you know who you are, then you know exactly who you are. You observe and react to the situations of others who need your help. You think of others and help them deal with different situations in their life.

Practice forgiveness

Holding grudges is not good for yourself or even others. It creates hostility. Forgiveness improves the quality of your life. You became aware of other people's feelings. Lastly, you deal with people in a better way.

Be mindful

Whatever you do, your actions and feelings, you need to be aware of people living around you. Be polite and calm. This will connect with people more and enhance your happiness

Affirm regularly

Every morning in the mirror, tell yourself that you are an important person and you are able. Affirmation improves yourself

self- awareness. You even start appreciating those in your environment more.

Listen more, talk less
People love being listened to. Let people rant about their problem to you, and you can offer them solutions. Or rather a shoulder to lean on

Think before you act
You need to be fully aware before speaking or answering a question. Some answers can be offending, so always try to be careful.

Make yourself better
Every day you should be competing with yourself. You ought to strive to be a better person than you were yesterday. So each minute tries to better yourself. The following are some ways to achieve this:

Go offline

Try it for a month, and you wouldn't regret it. Social media has a lot of noise. Being offline will not only help you love yourself but also appreciate you more?

Observe
The world has numerous opportunities. It awaits people to take advantage of such situations. Learn from the mistake, choose wisdom from the words of people you admire, come up with ideas from your evening walk. You just need to do is open your eyes and see.

Read
Read a lot. Books, newspapers, magazines, and blogs. There is lots of information on your books which helps you improve yourself. The best part is you can choose any genre you want. Do you love technology, health, or travel then go for it. With time your knowledge of things will improve.

Stop procrastination

This is a killer of dreams. Just rise from that comfy situation and dare to become. Do you doubt yourself? You can.

Help others
You wouldn't know how this will make other people smile. Small acts like helping an older man to cross the road, or opening a door for someone is not only fulfilling to you but also the other person.

Surprise people
It could be you, workmate, friend, or parent. Make a smile on people's faces. They need it. People will love you and appreciate you more.

Writing
Write about anything. It could be to create your day, a person you admire and adore. Writing helps you cultivate discipline. You'll want to practice your skill daily.

Compliment yourself.

You are beautiful and smart. Compliment yourself every day and congratulate yourself on the little achievements that you make.

Practical examples

Emotional intelligent takes a massive part in our daily activities and your workplace.

How people conduct themselves in a meeting

Meeting where everyone talks and they aren't listening to each other can be chaotic. Hence, reflecting people's ego. But, when one person speaks at a time, then, evidently, people are listening to each other. EQ is at plays a role in this. It just shows how people have respect and care about the other party's emotions.

People expressing themselves in an office

When people can express themselves openly, without being hindered is a practical example of EQ. This depicts their feelings, views, and opinions is important to the organization. The exchanges should be in a respectful manner.

Organizations, where the employees are free to speak out, are pleasant. When search issues are rated out, an emotionally intelligent boss wouldn't be offended bit would instead take affirmative action and congratulate the person for being free.

Flexibility

Emotionally intelligent people have a warm heart. They know that they work with human beings and nit machines. They would instill strict rules on the work environment. Instead, they understand that people are different and respect their work as long as the job is done.

Freedom and space to be creative

Organizations should create room for creativity. Refusing people the idea is not only unethical but also terrible. When a superior suppresses one thought, then it can only show that their emotional quotient is low.

There is compassion
Arguments, in homes, workplaces usually occur. Dealing with people's mood swings, changed attitude says a lot about your EQ level. Being able to understand that a person's mood is terrible, and responding to the other person calmly is equally important when an employee fails to do their work well, then, the leader should think before scolding him and throwing hurtful words to them. They should motivate them and encourage them to work hard. The result will enhance teamwork.

Interacting out of work hours
Interacting during lunch breaks, chatting on the corridors, catching a bus after work

shows social behavior. Social activities ensure that people have funned, share their joyful moments, and also their sorrowful moments. Thus, they bond. This depicts how emotionally intelligent they are, and connect with other people and create social interactions.

Developing emotional quotient personally
When you are upset or angry, and you show it on yourself, then this will likely push people away from you. Learning how to control your emotions would make you friendlier.
You need to have self-awareness and self-cautious be to achieve this. Then use self-regulation to develop emotional quotient.
Learning to calm is important since it doesn't influence our decision-making process.

Chapter 7: Brief Description Of Emotional Intelligence

When you hear the words 'Emotional Intelligence', what exactly comes to your mind? Do you ever doubt yourself for what you think? Now think about this. You find yourself in a group of arrogant people, and you have to deal with them because this is something that needs your attention and effort. Do you leave this task undone because your partners are arrogant, and you can't stand them? What do you do?

Now, this is it. Emotional Intelligence is something psychological. It involves understanding your own emotions and the ones of the people that you interact with from home, school, church, work or any other circumstance. An emotionally intelligent person will know how to handle every kind of character they meet. Asking why? The knowledge of psychology will allow you to read through the mind of someone you are interacting with and helps you to identify their state of emotions. When you understand the emotions of the people around you, working with them becomes easier because you will be in a position to deal with them without hurting their feelings and also not being too selfish to your own emotions.

Let's take an example of a situation where you want a vacant position in the Students' Union in your college. You will have to start at some point. First, you have to believe in yourself that you can do this. Then know the people you want to deal with. Remember, you need votes, and for other people to vote for you, you have to convince them that you were able to serve their interests without favoring anyone or taking everything to yourself. You have to campaign and present yourself to the voters to let them know you better and how you will be working with them. They need to know the services you will deliver to them, so this must be made clear by you. You need to know their mind and what they like for you to convince them that you are going to deliver exactly what they need.

When you are emotionally intelligent, you will be in a position to serve their interests at the expense of your own emotions, and this is normally because no one can vote in a person who is against their interests. All you need is the votes, and your psychology will make it clear to you that once you show someone, you can deliver what they need, winning their votes will not be a task anymore. All you have to do is play their game, win their cards then influence them to the direction you were heading to.

Emotional Intelligence walks with us everywhere. It is that feeling that makes you understand someone easily and take advantage of their personality to serve your interest without hurting them. Emotional Intelligence keeps everything easy for you. How does this work? It helps you to understand the kind of people you are interacting with. When misunderstandings arise, you will be able to solve everything without nagging because you can easily control your audience without any of them knowing your motive. It helps you out of traps that can easily lead to your failure.

For the case of a speaker, emotional intelligence is what makes you move your audience easily and engage them in your speech. It enables you to identify what can offend your audience and avoid it. It is the same emotional intelligence that will enable you to know whether your audience is active or not and how you can balance between your emotions and the emotions of your audience to keep them attentive and make them enjoy every bit of your speech.

Emotional Intelligence gives a solution to every problem. You must be asking 'how.' This is it. Anyone who understands the psychology of emotions cannot want to engage in endless fights when at the back of their mind they know very well that they can hold their emotions for a while to attend to other people peacefully and use unclear tactics to control the emotions of others and influence them to come to one agreement that they have been longing for.

Advocates apply emotional intelligence to rule in their favor. They use the techniques of dark psychology to control the audience and influence them to accept their rulings without raising eyebrows. They make the audience to believe that what they say is right and that no one should doubt their decisions. To them, they get exactly what they want, but still, they don't do it in a way that makes others feel that they have been denied their rights.

Emotional Intelligence works in a way that is not easy for any rare person to understand. In most cases, it is used by those in power to get themselves what they want. They easily manipulate other people to win every game of the mind. They are made to understand other people's thoughts and control them silently without showing any signs of manipulation. Their knowledge of emotions allows them to get in line with everyone, enjoy their trip and win them to take a different direction than wasn't their interest.

Emotional Intelligence is what makes everything work the way they are needed. You cannot convince anyone to perceive a new idea without winning their minds. In everything you do, especially when it comes to sales, you need to understand what other people like, and also have the power to convince them that your product is the best for them even if it is not.

Every salesperson is a manipulator. For them to convince their customers to purchase their products over and over again, they need to be emotionally stable. It is the rule of every business. It is what makes any sales successful and attracts more customers. When you are able to identify your customers' needs, you are able to keep them and provide everything that satisfies their needs without sacrificing your own needs.

That's how Emotional Intelligence works everywhere. It goes hand in hand with mind control, and if you understood the above concepts well, you are pretty good to handle anything that comes your way.

Chapter 8: Channeling The Right Energy For Healing

What There Is to Know

The human mind is a work of complex perfection. It works in a way that even modern studies till this day have not fully been able to comprehend. Some would say this is the reason we underestimate the power of our intuitive personalities, which, for the most part, are responsible for our "constructive reasoning."

When we stay connected to the energy around us, we work in sync with our inner bodies - that is, the spiritual, mental, and emotional parts of our being. It's like plugging in your television. As long as it stays plugged in, the TV continues to work. That's the way it is for us. We have to work with the energy around us for us to be able to work on actively healing ourselves and others.

You do not have to be glued to a tree to connect to nature's energy field. It's in the air we breathe. This connection can be established when we are in the same vicinity as the source of energy or even across a whole universe!

It all depends on the energy force. We are created to be attracted to this energy force. We all have this energy within. In fact, we are made of the same energy. That is why sometimes, you feel stifled and you tell yourself you need a breath of fresh air. That is just you seeking to re-establish your connection with nature's energy force. This connection is not just about quantum physics. It's about maintaining the energy balance on Earth, because if we cause an imbalance, we may disrupt the pattern of energy flow.

However, there is more to channeling healing power than just connecting to nature's energy field. Let's go back to the television we spoke about earlier. Now that you have connected it to the energy source, why don't you sit in front of it to watch something? You may say, "*I am not dumb,I know it's switched off!*" So put it on!

That's exactly what we also need as empaths. To channel that healing power, we have to put our energy force on! Not just leave it connected, but to actually activate it! In so doing, we can channel it and transfer it to others, thereby commencing their healing process. There are a lot of ways to do that, but whichever method you choose, simplicity is the key!

Why People Pray

I try as much as possible to be broad minded and never question anybody's religion, but I would really love to ask you an odd question. Okay, here it is: Why do you think people pray?

You might say it's because they believe in a supreme being that can attend to their needs and heal them, but let me tell you what I think.

I think people pray because it works for them. What they do not know is that they are unconsciously channeling energy through their prayers. This is what some spiritual empaths would call "affirmations." Saying it and making it happen. It's like directing that activated energy to do or change something.

Remember I said everything has its own energy. So through that maintained connection they have, they communicate, and they channel the energy toward their desired end. Some people pray repeatedly to make that thing happen for them, or to get healed of a particular disease. Then they wait through "faith."This waiting period is how long it takes for your internal energy to communicate with the energy around you through an already pre-established connection.

Like I said before, this is what I think, and it is what works for me. I channel that power and it can do anything for me. It is not too different from the religious command to "believe" in what is not seen. Because this sort of energy is not the sort to be seen with the physical eye.

So, what do you think? Could this be another level in human development? I feel it is. I feel our lives are not just based on the physical. We are spiritual beings. It's evident in the little things. The little things that science can't and hasn't explained. In the things that our complex human minds can't comprehend.

It is not unexpected then that prayers or positive reasoning is a shared factor in many religions. In a responsive universe, the intensity of prayers and positive intuition originate from associating with our true nature. I am sure you have heard someone say at some point that the universe is listening. It actually is!

All aspects of life is just energy that has been moderated to a certain vibration called "subtle energy," making it just that much easier for it to travel around, through people, animals, and things. This energy is normally transmitted out into the world, affecting all electromagnetic energy fields. *You must have already known that, but it's good to be sure.*

Also, these teeny tiny energies can be directed internally - that is, inside you - creating harmony from the inside out, treating you, and easing your pain. Think of them as micro-chips, each with its specific function. Meditation and Reiki are perfect examples of this type of treatment. Through different sorts of thoughts and prayers, we can take positive thoughts and channel them into potential positive results. This is a type of treatment that works for a lot of people - mostly the religious and/or spiritual ones. *We are walking balls of good energy and this energy is like playdough. We can mold it in infinite ways, and get infinite results. How cool is that?*

Centering our energy helps us free ourselves from emotional, mental, and spiritual restraints. It's like conjuring a ball of light, and as it expands, it eliminates every speck of darkness around us, helping us accept the past and forget a better future.

When we channel the wrong energy, probably when we are around chaotic environments filled with hatred, anger, and frustration, we invoke negativity. This affects everything we do. It messes up our emotions, compromises our already established connections to energy forces around us, and makes us feel like crap.

Keep It Positive!

So, focus this channeled energy into bringing positive results into your life. Because, if you are going to heal anybody, channeling negative energy will do more harm than good, and you don't want that. It will hurt you too, because as an empath, you can't help but suffer alongside your patient.

Positive energy rules the universe. This positive energy has been an overwhelming power lighting up humankind since the start of humanity. Throughout the hundreds of years, the idea of energy has had numerous names. For instance, the Japanese call it "Ki," the Chinese call it "Chi," the Indians call it "Prana," and the Greek refer to it as "Aether." The Universe is an extending heap of energy that blends and structures new energy from old energy. I am sure we were all thought in science class that energy can neither be created nor destroyed, but can be transferred from one form to another. It is all around us!

For instance, stars in the night sky pass on and breathe out their worn out gases to shape nebulae, the origination of new stars. Life and passing, in vast terms, comprises a rotative cycle. Positive energy depends on the result of this cycle. *We are energy. Everything around us is energy, and on some level or the other, whether physical or spiritual, we relate to this deeply.*

Whatever is placed out into the world, will come back to the fountain of energy. Positive energy moves through the air we inhale like undetectable swells on a calm lake. This energy is the fuel we need to carry out our daily activities. I do not mean this in basic terms like what we eat and such. I mean this on a deeper level. It beats through the universe as gases that structure both far off worlds and the charged particles of lightning that hit our terraces on a stormy night.

By directing our thoughts through positive reasoning, we produce another energy fit for producing positive responses which will travel through our surroundings dependent on the quantum logical laws of the Universe.

The good thing about all this is that energy is straightforward. We are all connected with one another in one way or the other through a network of energy and matter. Each activity we partake in, each word we speak, and each demonstration of empathy or evil is entwined in ways that rise above our presence here on Earth.

We are a part of this wholeness that is the Universe. Also, with such greatness comes the responsibility to live well and be loving individuals. This is why you have to live well, love frequently and be benevolent to yourself as well as other people.

Loving yourself as an empath is one of the best things you can do. It may seem as if you are not in control of who you are because of the different emotions that course through you, but you are your own being! Your emotions are your own! So stay grounded.

All Is Energy

Everything is comprised of energy and everything is associated with and by energy. Energy turns out to be "good" or "bad" depending on the way we are affected by it. It is our impression of the aftereffects of this concept which our psyches accept as either positive or negative. Be that as it may, the energy itself is a characteristic articulation of the universe itself.

We can change the way a circumstance makes us feel, regardless of whether we are able to change it or not. We can program our self to realize that if we do "A," the result would be "B." For instance, I know I will get burnt if I pour boiling water on my hand. *It's just a simple case of actions and consequences!*

There are sensible results to each move that we make, regardless of whether that activity is simply considering it, discussing it, or very much acting on it..

Manifesting Favourable Conditions

It is unimaginable to expect to live in some Utopian dream where nothing ever turns out badly. We do have the ability to impact our environment and be the draftsmen of our own lives. So, why don't we do anything about it?

To be the recipient of such great and positive energy is perfect in physical reality. In fact, we would be happier if we were able to predict the results of some of our actions and thoughts.

An irrefutable truth is that we bring into reality what we always think about. It's called "mind over matter." Scientists have tried to discover how this works, but have been unsuccessful in doing so. What they have noticed is that patients who put a conscious effort into feeling better actually heal faster than those who are exhausted and have lost hope. It's energy! And it manages the results of everything we do.

In that vein, thinking positively gets increasingly positive results, and thinking negatively gets progressively negative results. What I mean is to concentrate on what you need and focus on turning it into a reality. That does not mean wallowing in denial when something negative is going on in your life. But! Don't spend all your energy agonizing over what you know you can't change!

Just pack your emotional bags and envision yourself away from that abusive emotion or feeling. Give yourself a little pep talk. If you did something wrong, just say "Well, I learnt not to do that again, and so I have I made progress.' 'If you did something you were not supposed to do, don't despair. Just tell yourself, " I know now what i didn't then, so I will be more careful in the future."

You have to forgive yourself,that's all that matters!

How to Channel More Positive Energy into Your Life

Be thankful.

Be consistently thankful for what you have. Concentrate on delivering a genuine sentiment of appreciation when offering your thanks. Try to write what you are thankful for everyday in a book or journal.Try to write everyday, so whenever you have a bad day, you could always go through all you were thankful for in the previous days. It will go a long way toward easing your mind. Try to write something different each day, so as to avoid daily repetitions.

You could even write a list of what made you genuinely happy at the end of each day!

If you were happy for helping an old man across the street, write it!
As an empath, it's easy to derive joy from the little things around you, so,be thankful!

If you keep writing what you are thankful for,before long, you would start to appreciate it and your subconscious will begin to accept it.

Be mindful of what you open yourself to
Get a lid on what you allow yourself to be exposed to when engaging with the media. Being always assaulted with negative pictures and boisterous forceful music does not produce a positive and clean energy.

Be careful of the company you keep
Be careful about the general population and conditions around you. Keep your condition as positive as could reasonably be expected. Toxic company will just drag you down.

Encircle yourself with constructive friends, people who really like you for who you really are, and who don't put unreasonable pressure on you. A lot of times, we stop listening to our intuition and listen to negative advice we get from other people. What you should bear in mind is that the negative counsel they give is really a reflection of their own fears and doubts. Also, the energy from a constructive relationship can be positively infectious. Continuously tune in to your Heart and Soul. Keep in mind that the intensity of your thoughts will open your concealed potential.

It's All About the Energy

Antiquated societies comprehended that we live in an immense ocean of energy. They understood that the planets and stars are cognizant creatures who speak with one another. They accepted that the trees fill in as radio wires, which enable normal unobtrusive energies and data to stream up from the Earth to the stars and planets, and from all other divine bodies into the Earth.

They made us understand that everything and each being has cognizance and channels this energy as they are able to, depending on their knowledge and ability in channeling energy.

Once we are better at channeling positive energy, the existing power of the Earth and universe moves through us all the more easily. Our abilities become enhanced and we begin to do things we would have found difficult to do before. Take healing, for example. If you work on your channeling ability, you will discover that you find it easier to infuse positive energy into a sick person.

In regards to yourself,you will notice that you have increased innovativeness, extrasensory discernment, and the ability to achieve physical and emotional healing. Shamans have figured out how to feel, sense and use this energy without separating or deforming it. They regularly allude to this procedure as turning the energy into an "empty bone."

We Are Responsible for Energy Flow

This widespread ocean of energy, Chi, Prana or whatever you'd rather call it, circles through our bodies, connects with the electromagnetic range, and incorporates other subtle energies not yet comprehended by Western science. It is what led to acupuncture, where needles are used to help the progression of essential energy through nerves in the body.

The Hopis of the American Southwest use the term "Kachina" to depict the universe of subtle energies. They perform customs and functions to associate with the

Kachina so as to pull in a rush of energy to develop their yields, and to get healing and many other things.

The Dogon people of Africa consider the channel through which the Earth ventures energies through us, the Bayuali. They call the channel through which we get energies from the universe, the Yenu. The Dogon accept that it is our duty as people to be clear channels who facilitate the progression of huge energy forces instead of meddling with or blocking them.

Although western medication limits its concentration to electromagnetic energies, it acknowledges that the human body works as a two-way radio wire. Specialists use instruments, - for example, ECG's and EEG's - to decide if a patient is as yet alive by estimating the electrical energy being transmitted from inside that patient's body. They know that our bodies get data from electromagnetic fields in our bodies to manage the circadian rhythms of our bodies.

Scientific investigations show that the spinal line (containing cerebro-spinal liquid which is conductive) serves as a means of reception, and that DNA fills in as a fractal receiving wire, used for working at a wide range of frequencies. *I know this may seem a bit geeky, but it's fascinating!*

It is likewise fascinating to take note of the fact that the U.S. armed forces showed that trees fill in as astoundingly great radio wires for remote correspondence and used them for this very purpose during the Vietnamese War.

EEG studies performed on normal meditators showed that they were prone to enter a phase of brainwave function called the "theta phase." Those who meditate regularly report a considerable shift in their energy field, a heightened sense of knowing, visions, as well as emotional and physical healing.

As an empath, regular meditation can get you to this theta phase of unconscious superiority. Think about it. You could be the hero the world needs, thanks to the healing you can offer from this theta phase of brainwave function!

Another very straightforward approach to give healing energy is to channel it from the ethereal plane, the process is called ethereal conditioning. So what is this ethereal conditioning? It's the wellspring of healing energy. In different places, it has been known as a grid, an egregore, a group, or The Universe. *It's like having your own store room filled with enough energy which you can always tap into whenever the need arises.*

Ethereal conditioning is like a very useful and handy device. A steady, enduring structure made of energy that relates with the brain.

This process I am about to outline might seem too simple to be true, but remember what I said about prayers earlier? So, make it work for you! Just like learning something new, the process might seem a bit foreign to you in the beginning. Just take it one bit at a time and try not to rush everything at once.

Rather, since it might seem a bit new to you, practice it until you get the hang of it. Do this frequently for at least a week, at which point you may perfect it. So to start, you should focus on stages one and two until you perfect them, then start again from stages one to three until you feel comfortable with that too, before you move forward. Then you can move on to practice everything together.

What to Do

Use your mind's eye

So first of all, you need to close your eyes, breathe deeply and calm yourself.

I know that may seem impossible while you read this, so why don't you read through the steps first, then when you are sure you know what you are supposed to do, go back to calming yourself without any distractions.

When you are sure that you are calm and your breathing is regular, try to locate that point of pain or discomfort internally. What I mean is that your eyes should still be closed, but let your internal eye travel over your body and find the source of pain. Some who have perfected this process say that they are even able to see this place in a different hue than the rest of the body, in their mind's eye. Now that you have located the site of discomfort, the ethereal conditioning will mark this location to mark your aim.

Just think of it as trying to shoot a target. Of course you won't be able to do that if you don't know where your target is at in the first place!

Draw in your mind

The ethereal conditioning will inspect the location you have targeted, and in a way determine what needs to be done. *After all, in a logical sense, you can't possibly just slap a strip of sticky tapes on an open wound, can you?* This is what the ethereal conditioning does: it helps us gauge the level of damage, and figures out what is needed to fix it.

In this step, you would need to draw in your mind. In other words, find your point of energy. As spiritual healers say,our energy source can be found at the center of our beings.

So draw into yourself and imagine being in a totally dark room, with your external environment being very far away from you. Tune out any noise around you and level your breathing.

When you are done with that, envision a speck of light in all that darkness. Imagine this little speck of light growing steadily around you until your whole internal world is illuminated.

When you illuminate this ethereal space, try to maintain this energy, because any sort of distraction can break your balance and let the light dwindle out.

Channelling the energy

In the event that you have given your ethereal conditioning a name, you could call upon it and direct it to travel the length of your body. Envision it coursing the length of your body, as if using its hands to locate the point you targeted in the first step. Like I said before, if you have perfected the previous two steps, you should see your body in a certain hue, probably from a faint pink hue to a vibrant red. So, any abnormality would normally have an odd hue that does not quite fit in with the rest of the colors. This odd color ranges from a dull grey hue, to black in some very serious conditions.

Put your hands around the injury

If you find this spot internally in your ethereal environment, put your hands around the injury physically. Try to apply a little pressure on the spot. Mind you, all these steps can work as well for other people as they work for you. It's the same thing. If this point of discomfort is not fixed, let your hand drift over the whole expanse of skin that needs healing. Mind you, this process is in no way related to open wounds and bleeding injuries. While you might be able to reduce the person's pain, this process won't heal that kind of injury.

Start diverting the energy

With your hands on the injury, start to divert the energy you channeled in your ethereal space to the site of injury. If done properly, you should feel the skin beneath your hands get warmer as the energy courses through the body to get to that point. Make sure you do not get distracted at this point because you might irrevocably hurt yourself or the person you may be trying to heal. Do not despair if this doesn't work right away, this is a process that you can easily repeat, and can be done at anytime of day.

Chapter 9: Building Self Protection – How To Protect Yourself From Manipulative People

Psychological manipulation is the exertion of excessive and unwarranted emotional influence over others while putting the victim at a disadvantage.

It is emotional exploitation that leads to mental distortion and loss of emotional intelligence and independence. The victim becomes emotionally dependent on the manipulator who, in return, derives satisfaction from the control and privileges that come with the lopsided relationship. Unlike healthy social relationships that are constructive and rewarding for both parties, psychological manipulation is founded on parasitism. The victim's energy and their essence of being are sucked by the manipulator; an energy vampire. Psychological manipulators are driven to a wide range of complex issues ranging from their own personal experiences to mental distortion. In some cases, such individuals have been conditioned by the environment especially family settings. Without proper intervention, children who grow up in emotionally abusive environments tend to normalize such behaviors as adults. They, in turn, become manipulative. Moreover, living in an emotionally toxic environment makes individuals vulnerable to accept emotional abuse from manipulators. However, the problem is usually deep-seated, and their manipulative behaviors are indicators of how deep the problem goes.

Humans are emotional beings – we tend to seek emotional validation from friends, families, and even in some extreme cases, total strangers. Whether good or bad, these emotions are important when it comes to establishing and fostering social relationships at home, school, or workplace. However, such a mighty power of emotions can be easily exploited by manipulative individuals. Such individuals are adept at manipulating people emotionally for their own gain while concealing their ulterior motives. They use emotive situations to control an emotionally vulnerable individual while masking their true intentions with a destructive hammer disguised as a helping hand. Manipulative individuals have psychopathic tendencies such as lack of empathy and impulsivity. They draw gratification and validation from manipulating and holding others back from outgrowing their cycle of influence. With almost genius-level mastery of the art of flip flopping on issues, emotionally manipulative people are cunning individuals who also find a way of adapting to new scenarios to suit their needs. Therefore, ditching them can be a Herculean task, especially for empaths who are emotionally sensitive and prone to emotional manipulation. Emotionally controlling individuals easily pounce on the naturally giving character of empaths to redirect attention to themselves at the opportune moment. Therefore, it is imperative for empaths to build self-protection against manipulative people.

The first step towards building self-protection against chronically manipulative people is identifying such individuals through their characteristics. Individuals who thrive on negative psychological influence are distinguished by their ability to detect other people's weaknesses, especially emotional vulnerabilities. They are skillful at identifying individuals who are more likely to fall into their well-laid trap. Manipulative people are predatory; they target the seemingly weak prey within the larger social community. Whether within the family, workplace, or any social and professional gathering, individuals with chronic manipulative tendencies have the cunning ability to offer support and help for individuals who are emotionally distressed. After zeroing in on their target, the psychological violation and exploitation begin. The terrible scheme hatched by manipulative people is aimed at convincing their victims that they are the bad guys. They create and nurture the notion that their victims are on the wrong side. Words will be twisted and actions tailored towards their vile agenda.

Being on the receiving end of such well-calculated emotional aggression can be overwhelming and outright confusing for many people. But such onslaught is aimed at cracking an individual's will and perseverance. When not stopped, the victim will surrender the controls to the manipulator with the hopes of finding reprieve. Psychologically manipulative individuals herd their victims towards an emotional island. They then create a sense that the only two inhabitants of the island are the victim and the manipulator. Therefore, the victim readily accepts the deadly tentacles disguised as help. The helping hand offered progressively transforms into a deadly python-like grip. They will relentless squeeze the victim and drain them emotionally. In some cases, the victim is unaware that life is being snuffed out of them by such an individual. However, handing over the reins of control is the beginning of a downward spiral whose nadir is emotional desolation.

Such lack of awareness is common among empaths whose emotional vulnerability disadvantages them when it comes to dealing with chronically manipulative individuals. Attuned to absorbing emotions of different kinds from others, empaths are capable of bottling even extreme emotions without necessarily seeking for an emotional outlet. They take in even extreme negative emotions. Moreover, they are introverts and would rarely share their experiences with others. They limit their social circles to small groups of people. Empaths also tend to minimize the time they spend on social gatherings. These characteristics attract energy vampires like manipulative people.

Chronically manipulative individuals are shrewd are developing machinations for feeding on the weaknesses of their victims. They use such weaknesses as a weapon against the emotionally vulnerable individuals to their advantage. The primary objective of such machinations to redirecting a victim's energies towards the manipulative individual's self-centered interests. The victims losses their self-worth and sense of self-esteem. Serving the self-centered interests of the manipulator is the sole target of emotional exploitation and abuse by chronically manipulative individuals. Success to them is measured by close their victims are driven over the edge. They derive power, pleasure, and authority when their victims are hanging on the edge or writhing down in the valley below. When left unchallenged and unchecked, manipulators turn their victims into their puppets and can drive them self-harm. It is not uncommon for individuals who have emotionally abused to entertain suicidal thoughts, especially when they discover that they have been under a manipulative spell. Self-injuries such as slitting or wrist may precede even more ominous problematic and compulsive behaviors such as substance abuse, alcoholism, and even suicide. With introverted inclinations, empaths may resort even to even greater degrees of social and physical exclusion.

Self-Protection Against Sneaky Psychologically Manipulative People

After successfully understanding how chronic manipulative people operate, including their characteristics and their sole objective, it is imperative to learn how to build effective self-protection against such individuals. The key to building a successful self-protection wall around you as an empath understands two fundamental issues. First, chronically manipulative individuals thrive in the chaos created by negative emotions. They feed on such situations and derive happiness, power, and authority from them. They function by spinning the wheels of psychological manipulation. Therefore, they have well-crafted machinations to identify their victims and adapt their behaviors to lure emotionally vulnerable individuals.

Secondly, the problem is not your emotional vulnerability and sensitivity. The problem lies with the psychotic behaviors of manipulative wheel spinners. However, manipulative individuals would readily and incessantly convince you that the problem is you. It is the first step towards turning someone into an emotional puppet devoid of self-worth. They deconstruct an individual's sense of being and wire a hot stream of doubt through their spine. They become emotionally dependent on their would-be emotional tormentor. After turning their victims into empty shells, manipulative people fill the created void with baseless ideas aimed at promoting their self-centered agenda. Psychological manipulation is essentially slavery of the mind where the manipulator is the master, and the victim becomes the slave. The victim is deprived of peace, love, and harmony which are essential recipes for self-determination and enjoyment of the abundance of life.

The process of becoming an emotional puppet begins with subtle inroads. The first step towards protecting yourself against manipulative people is identifying these traps and avoiding them. To get under your skin and toy with your emotions, manipulative people deploy a wide range of cunning tactics. Ordinary and seemingly harmless questions and comments can be tailored to lure you into the trap. Manipulative people also use confusion to snare their unsuspecting victims. In some cases, they play with the mindset of their victims by guilt-tripping them. Blaming an emotionally vulnerable individual for a mishap can destabilize them psychologically. Consequently, they become easy pickings for calculating manipulator. On the surface, some of these tactics seem well-intentioned. An unsuspecting empath would readily give in to the interrogations and in some cases, accept reasonability for a mishap. However, hidden beneath the mundaneness of these actions are vile intentions aimed at micromanaging the emotional status of the victim leading to emotional submission and subjugation.

Avoid these emotional traps; it is advisable to understand your fundamental rights as a fully functional human being. Psychologically manipulative people pounce on self-doubt and inability of the victims to recognize when their fundamental rights are trampled upon by others. Forfeiture of these rights, for any particular reason, creates a vacuum that manipulators always seek to fill with their ill-motive ideas. Therefore, recognize and defend your right to hold and express a different opinion. This will give you a high sense of control and safeguard against being guilt-tripped by manipulators. Avoid the temptation of trooping with the masses in the hope that it would make you less weird. Holding a divergent opinion is the hallmark of self-determination. It will set you apart yet wholesome. Expressing your opinion especially as an empath, will rebuff the manipulators who find individuals too strong-willed to manipulate psychologically.

Upholding and safeguarding other individual fundamental rights such as the right to be respected and prior setting can keep off the unwanted attention by manipulators. Individuals who understand their need to be respected and can set their priorities can easily turn down the unwanted overtures from chronic manipulators. They stand by their 'no' decisions and answers and do not budge even when enticed by the energy vampires out to drain them emotionally. Moreover, they readily recognize tell-tale signs of mental, physical, or emotional abuse and exploitation. Being on the lookout for such threats discourages emotion puppeteers who prey upon the vulnerabilities and gullibility of others. By safeguarding these liberties, a would-be victim establishes a boundary that keeps out manipulators. Boundaries give an individual to self-appoint themselves leadership supremacy in their lives. Having the moral authority and power to shape your emotions and the general direction of your life is one of the surest ways of keeping manipulative people at bay. Self-assuredness eliminates doubts which manipulators use to cause confusion in the lives of their victims. Individuals who are self-assured are masters of their emotions and have moral authority in deciding the direction of their lives. You can easily set off the emotional traps laid by the manipulators without necessarily getting trapped when you have control over your life.

Secondly, many people fall into the chocking grasp of manipulators because of indecision and passive-aggression. The inability to stand firm against manipulative people is partly due to the flip flopping behaviors of manipulators. Psychologically manipulative people have perfected the skill of tinkering on the extremes leading to confusion among their victims. Blowing hot and cold on issues ensures that they keep their victims dazed long enough to trap them. It is not uncommon for a manipulator to show heart-warming kindness and politeness to one individual and still be unsympathetic to the plight of another. Manipulators habitually flow by the popular emotional waves. They can be aggressive or passive and helpless, depending on the situation and audience. All these tactics are aimed at entrapping emotionally vulnerable and sensitive individuals.

Sometimes all you may need is a writing pad and pen to note down key points of your conversation to keep track of their wavering opinions, statements, and actions. This is especially advisable once you notice their habitual oscillation between being sympathetic and unsympathetic. From seemingly plausible excuses and justifications to erratic behaviors and viewpoints, identify the patterns in their behaviors and actions. When you constantly remind them of their original stands and statements, manipulators will find you difficult as prey and shy away. Keeping track of manipulators' views and actions not only discouragement but also acts as a shield against falling into their traps. The surest way to set off a trap from a safe distance is by identifying it first.

Therefore, avoid being passive-aggressive when dealing with manipulators. Call them out forthwith once you realize their actions and words are ill-intentioned. As soon as you spot manipulators, actively deal with them, and they will flee from you. Even though they are masters of arm-twisting people emotionally and psychologically, even manipulators feel discouraged when their manipulative feelers are rebuffed or knocked back by their intended victims. Being actively aggressive in calling out manipulative people can prevent you from becoming their emotional toys. Standing up for the truth even when you are met with their wrath including denying their behaviors, will ensure that you rest easy knowing that you kept an emotional puppeteer at bay. Even when they turn the situation back on you and paint you as the bad person, do not flinch; hold fast to the truth, and they will finally give up. The immediate feeling of discomfort that they create by turning the situation back at you or even denying the whole incident will fade after a short time. However, the joy of protecting yourself will last for a very long time. It might even encourage others to stand up against such manipulative individuals especially at home, workplace or even within the community. And most importantly, pretending that what they are doing to is okay is dangerous. It might set a precedent for others who may fall victim to manipulators.

Manipulators stalk their victims with the view of identifying any signs of weakness. When they detect any weaknesses, they manipulate the situation either by blowing it out of proportion or turning it against their victims. The key to successful emotional manipulation by manipulative people is to make their intended victims feel bad about themselves. By planting seeds of doubt in the minds of their victims, manipulators will go to a great length to nurture and water the seeds to sprout and grow into full-blown self-hatred. An individual wallowing in self-pity and self-blame will feel inadequate and becomes emotionally dependent on others for validation. In most cases, manipulators will present themselves as the safest pair of hands to help them during such times. Buoyed by the false sense of care exhibited by the manipulator, the emotionally susceptible and scarred victim will more likely surrender their free will, freedoms, and power to manipulators. Whether a conscious or unconscious decision, the move will take the victim down a path of destruction. Therefore, understanding yourself beforehand will ensure that you avoid the temptation to turn to self-blame and personalization of issues whenever something goes wrong.

As a self-protection strategy, understanding yourself extends beyond knowing your fundamental rights. It encompasses trusting yourself and establishing moral boundaries. When you understand yourself, you will realize that emotions, whether negative or positive, are necessarily not bad. Additionally, you will get to understand that emotions stem from an unconscious place, including our past experiences. We have little to no control over. Their fizzling is involuntary, but the most important thing is our ability to deal with them. Let no one convince you that you should feel miserable because of your emotions especially in the case of empaths who are emotionally sensitive. The problem does not lie with

129

you or your emotional sensitivities; rather, the problem is with the manipulators who want to blow your emotions out of proportion and make your despondent.

In every situation where you encounter an emotional manipulator, self-protect yourself by gauging whether how you are being treated meets your respect threshold. Examine the expectations and demands that the manipulator requires of you. If you feel, based on your understanding of self, that they are unbecoming and demeaning and inclined towards serving the self-centered interests of the manipulator, firmly and politely reject them. Set the standards of what is a reasonable expectation and curl the perpetrators of unreasonable expectations and block them from influencing you. Additionally, scrutinize the direction in which the relationship with any individual will take. Manipulators thrive on developing one-way relationships with all the benefits going to them. When employing the self-understanding strategy to self-protect yourself against psychologically manipulative individuals, it is imperative that you always understand the direction of the relationship. How you feel about the relationship is the key to measuring how well it suits your standards and moral compass. While such may be a difficult task for empaths to undertake considering their ability to absorb negative emotions from others, having a go at self-understanding have multiple rewards that extend beyond dealing with manipulative individuals.

The fourth self-protection strategy is leveraging time. Manipulators always ensnare emotionally vulnerable people by pressurizing them into making decisions. They prefer on-the-spot decisions since they are rushed and not carefully considered. Knowing that their victims are under great pressure due to their emotionally draining situation, manipulators always seek to push decisions to be made without much thought. Decisions made during the spur

131

of the moment primarily stem from emotions. Such decisions are rarely the product of rational thinking. The emotional wounds are still raw and fresh. At this point, the victim is emotionally vulnerable and more likely to self-blame and personalize the problem. A rushed decision is the manipulator's way of bringing their victims into their immediate influence. Like salesmen, manipulators will seek to seal the deal immediately. Om some cases, they prefer catching their victims off-guard. It is not uncommon for an emotional manipulator to give short deadlines or notices for their victims to accomplish an important and time-consuming task. Failure to abide by the notice or deadline can lead to criticism and manipulation. An emotional manipulator may also seek to gain an advantage over you by picking the wrong moment to ask important questions. Your lack of preparedness in such a situation is the chink in the armor that manipulators are looking for.

Leverage time by asking the manipulator to give you time to consider the request or question. This will give you time to think rationally and critically before making a decision. You can only understand the benefits and shortcomings of a relationship when you give your time to think objectively. Emotions tend to cloud judgment. Exercise leadership over your thought processes and mental faculties by postponing making critical decisions when under emotional pressure. Having time to think will help you in bargaining for equal respect and benefits in any relationship. Giving yourself time is also a great way to create separation from any form of influence he or she might have established from the onset. Manipulators thrive in a momentary lapse in rational thinking. When told to wait, they tend to impatient and shy off. They fear that by asking for time to think about their suggestions or questions, the victims will rationalize everything. This works to their disadvantage.

Once you request time to think, keep a safe distance from them. This is because manipulators can easily explain themselves back into the picture. They have ideas at their fingertips to explain things away. If you do not fully detach yourself from them after leveraging time, they can easily convince you to reconsider your stance. They can expertly excuse and justify even the most unfathomable of actions as long as their objective of putting you under their influence is achieved. For empaths who are renowned for their kind and forgiving hearts, they can easily find themselves at crossroads. They may absorb such excuses and justifications and be tempted to give in. However, their rational minds may tell them otherwise.

The fifth tip to consider when dealing with chronically emotionally manipulative people is founded on the concept of self-preservation. Prevent being trapped into the toxic web of manipulation by diplomatically and firmly confronting them. Concisely and effectively articulate your stand, priorities, and opinion without damaging the existing relationships with the manipulator. In most cases, manipulators are people close to us, either as workmates, family members, and friends. These are individuals we interact with frequently and avoiding physical contact with them can be challenging. Even emotionally manipulative workmates are important members of workplace teams. Keeping peace with these individuals may be a necessity due to circumstances. When met with low resistance, a firmly and tactfully said 'no' can foster a great understanding between the manipulator and would-be victim. It can also inspire others who have fallen victim to manipulation within the same environment to stand up and defend their rights and priorities without being guilt-tripped by manipulators. In the end, you end up preserving your peace while also enjoying greater emotional freedom.

Additionally, diplomacy while standing your ground will ensure that you handle manipulative people who become bullies safely. A physically confrontational situation pitying an emotionally sensitive and vulnerable victim against bully manipulators can easily turn ugly. Bullies are emotionally insecure and in most cases, are victims of bullying. Turning in bullying is one of the ways through which psychological manipulators try to make up or avenge their own sufferings. Therefore, bullying becomes a way of pulling others down to their level. When they cut you down emotionally, such individuals will feel a false and deranged sense of tallness and supremacy. Whether in the office, at home, or in the schoolyard, develop a spine and defend yourself against such bullies whose aim is to exert emotional control over you.

However, even as you stand for your fundamental rights, consider your safety first. Safety first is a pearl of old-age wisdom whose importance must be emphasized whenever one encounters a manipulator who is a bully. Ensuring your safety can be achieved by simple acts such as picking the right moment to stand up against a manipulator. Having people as a witness may deter the bully from becoming physically confrontational. Documenting incidences of bullying can also discourage bullies. A paper trail can provide enough evidence to have enough people in your corner to defend you, especially in work settings. You will realize that you are not alone in the fight. There is a wide range of professionals including law enforcement officers and counselors who can support you. By documenting and reporting any form of abuse to the concerned parties, you are standing up for yourself and calling out manipulators.

Another self-protection approach that requires tact and firmness is destabilizing their source of manipulative power. Manipulators exert influence because of the power they perceive they have over others. In work and domestic settings, such power manifests in the form of superior position or seniority, academic qualification, or possession of certain skills considered rare within the setting at the time. Additionally, manipulators who have control over certain resources within the workplace, home, or even community may draw their manipulative power from such a scenario. Others may even draw power from their social and professional connections. This may include co-workers, teammates, siblings, subordinates, influential leaders, and even friends. They will feel that people are beholden to them and, therefore, should bend to their will. In extreme cases, such manipulators may resort to physical and verbal abuse or bullying. They may feel untouchable because of the power they have over others.

The sources of power become the center of gravity of these people. Destabilizing this source of stability can tip the balance of power in favor of would-be victims and render manipulators powerless. To avoid confrontations while also being diplomatic, identify and strive to take away these centers of gravity. If your workmate is manipulating you because of a special skill they possess, take your time and learn the skill if possible. It will free you from having to operate within their circles of influence. Alternatively, scout for individuals with such skills and let them join the company. If necessary, make inroads into the manipulator's social circles without tipping him or her off. Having common allies will tone down their power. By taking their prized possession and the leverage they have over others, you will diminish their influence. Cut from their power source, manipulators refocus their energies away from trying to controlling others. Siphon power from manipulators is not only strategic; it also throws them off balance. It is a reality check for emotional puppeteers to realize that their would-be victims can match their hyped power and might.

Sometimes power is not derived from such associations and possessions. Manipulators are capable of exercising their dominance in physical places where they own or feel comfortable in. Such spaces can be their offices or even public spaces, including parks where they are familiar with. Such familiarity or ownership will give the manipulator an upper hand during conversations and negotiations. You are likely to feel less comfortable in physical spaces where a manipulator is bound to dominate mentally. Any transactions carried in such environments are inherently lopsided and favors the manipulator. To avoid finding yourself in such a situation of imbalanced power especially during negotiations and meetings, opt for neutral spaces. Home turf will give the manipulator the home advantage over you. However, negotiating or conversing in the manipulator's home turf is sometimes unavoidable. In case you find yourself in such a scenario, it is advisable to reset your bearings using icebreakers. These can be simple actions such as diversionary small talks or sharing a cup of coffee. Other people get their bearings by taking in their environment. A simple yet engaging talk on wall photos, paintings or hangings can take off the pressure on your shoulders. This can set the stage for a more balanced interaction instead of being controlled and manipulated.

Emotional manipulators are cunning characters who prey upon the vulnerabilities of their victims. Any emotional cracks, even the tiniest ones, are exploited and aggravated and turned into diabetic wounds. While such cracks are sometimes unavoidable, developing strategies to keep off toxicities from manipulators can prevent them from becoming diabetic. When emotionally charged, as sometimes is the case for empaths, engage in activities that will enable you to develop inner peace. Consider meditation to calm your nerves. Meditating will help you connect with higher realms and develop positive thoughts. A positive outlook of life keeps away manipulators who thrive in negativity. Emptiness attracts manipulators who will seek to feel the empty space with negative emotions to their own benefit. Meditation will help you make sense of the chaos that unfolds around and find calmness and purpose even in the most difficult situations. Meditation teaches a higher sense of loving kindness even in the face of hostility, which is a great way of avoiding physical confrontations with the manipulator. In most cases where the manipulator is driven by their dark past, resulting in compassion will disarm them. Your loving kindness can transform a manipulator into a genuinely kind and loving individual.

If you have not mastered the art of meditation, consider other options such as reading, exercising, or writing. These activities will enable you to release pent up emotions while also allowing you to zone out manipulators and negative thoughts. The benefits of these activities are manifold. Reading and writing are also a great way of learning new ideas, skills or even art to occupy your time. You develop professionally and personally while also keeping manipulators at bay. If your co-worker, sibling, or friend is always seeking to manipulate you because of a skill they possess; reading to ground yourself can be a great way to offset their power source and center of gravity. In addition to the health and physical benefits of exercising, you also stand to enjoy an improved mental status. Moreover, you get to meet new people, especially in gyms or parks. Group exercises might be a ticket to meeting new allies who will help you built a better social network. This will come in handy when a manipulator's power source is his or her friends.

While grounding yourself and zoning out unnecessary distractions can be an effective self-protection strategy against manipulators, it is always advisable to engage in constructive activities. Avoid the temptation of filling your time and emptiness with destructive activities such as gossiping and binging on television, food, or both. When emotionally hurt, filling up your brain with wild ideas and information propagated on television and social media can lead you to a path whose end is despair and feeling miserable. These are pointless activities that will make even more vulnerable to manipulation. Such information and activities will consume your time, leaving you purposeless and at the mercy of manipulators. They will distract you from your destiny and create a false sense of belonging. Always strive to keep in touch with reality.

Individuals who are staked down to one opportunity are easy pickings for manipulators. Emotionally vulnerable and sensitive people are easily boxed into staying in unproductive situations. From stale relationships to dead-end jobs, they may find such situations familiar and comfortable. They become emotionally attached to these jobs and relationships and even individuals. They lose their independence and become overly reliant on people, workplaces, and relationships. Upon the urging of other people, they develop a phobia of the unknown. Emotional manipulators easily identify individuals who are emotionally attached to their jobs, relationships or even places. In case the manipulator is your partner or workmate, they are more likely to steamroll over your emotions and use your attachment to confuse and exert undue influence and control over you.

By studying behavior patterns and understanding your fundamentals, assess how genuinely you are respected and treated in any relationship. When you realize that your emotions are ignored, manipulated, and steamrolled over, break away. However, be tactful and avoid confrontations. Remain cordial but emphasize that you value your emotional well-being; something that the current relationship setup is not currently offering. In some cases, it is advisable to cut off links with such manipulative individuals especially when they resort to physical, verbal or emotional abuse. Such individuals are incapable of sustaining a civil relationship founded on mutual respect. Be cautious from the onset of any relationship. Investing too much at the onset of a relationship is ill-advised.

Psychological manipulators will always try to convince you that depending on a single opportunity is attractive. They detest ambition. They champion for contentment; having all your eggs in one seemingly safe basket. However, the safety of this single basket has been set by them. They will gladly justify its safety by all means while trying to tear down any objections you raise. To them, it is normal and prudent to live in one location or work in the same job and position. Wanting anything else is risky, awkward, and even selfish. They will argue you're your actions are driven by pride. Phrases and questions like 'why fix it when it is working' become commonplace. In reality, they are afraid that your mind will awaken, and you will no longer fall within their circle of influence. Therefore, continuously seek new opportunities to better your life. Create new experiences by taking new jobs, fostering new relationships or even moving to new locations. You will become emotionally independent and happier. Be adventurous and witness manipulators flee from you.

Finally, psychologically manipulators always target people with baby mentality. If you are constantly letting people walk over you and later complain, you are a prime target for manipulators. Remember, manipulators are always seeking for the opportunity to get into your head and mess up with your thinking. Whether you blame them later for your troubles is of little consequence to them. They can readily deny your accusations or turn them against you. You can easily become a bad person when dealing with a manipulator. In some cases, they may resort to physical confrontation or bullying. Repeatedly over-trusting people and getting hurt is babyish. When you are fooled more than once, then you ought to be ashamed of yourself. Despite the existence of manipulative people, the burden of self-protection falls on you. You do not have the free pass to fall victim to manipulators just because they exist and are cunning. It is not the fault of the psychological manipulator for toying with your emotions; it is your responsibility to prevent them from turning you into a puppet. You take full credit for all your successes and failures; they define you.

People will always try to outthink you. They will come up with crafty ways to over-strategize you. Getting one over you is the primary goal of manipulators. If, upon assessment, you realize that an individual is habitually slippery and flip flopping on issues, do not hesitate to delete them from your life. Giving such individuals second chances is inviting trouble to your backyard. Be bold and cut loose people who you feel are trying to manipulate you emotionally. Having self-respect will ensure that you guard your dignity with jealousy.

Always bet on yourself, including your capabilities and intuition. If you have second thoughts about other's intentions, pull out or tread carefully. Hold yourself to higher standards. Make decisions based on both internal and external factors. And the most important internal factor and the only one you can control is yourself. External factors are beyond your control. Therefore, giving prominence to external factors will only leave you susceptible to manipulation. Shun empty promises. Challenge the status quo and carved out a life for yourself. Stop manipulators on their track by setting consequences for their actions. Babies have a nascent and gullible mentality. When you stop being a baby, you develop a strong mentality accompanied by a high sense of self-worth. Your capacity to take in negative emotions from manipulators without being affected will increase.

Chapter 10: The Persuasion

At this point, you have had some time to analyze the target and figure out what makes them tick. You know whether they are driven more by logic or by emotions, and you know a lot more about what will work as a technique of manipulation for them. Once you are done with that, it is time to move into planting some of the seeds of how you would like the target to behave. These are hopefully going to get the target to agree to your course of action, but they are planted in a manner that makes it so the target feels they got to make the decision, rather than them feeling like they are forced to make the decision by someone else.

When all of that is done, it is time to move on to the third part of influence the process of persuading people. This is going to be the part that will require you to bring in some physical actions, rather than just using your words. These physical actions are so important because they will really push things over the edge and will get your target to agree with you, or get them to comply, with the thing you are asking for.

The trick to this one is that you need to use persuasion in a way that is going to work on your target. This is where the other two parts come in. if you were successful with all of this, and you really worked towards making the target understood then you will find that the persuading part of all of this was pretty easy. You will be well equipped to deal with the target because you will know the perfect tactic of persuasion that you can use each and every time.

Persuasion is such an important part of this. And we are going to take some time to explore how to make this work and some of the different techniques that come with persuasion later on. But right now, remember that persuasion is going to be a big part of the manipulation, and it is the step that will help to seal the deal. If you are able to put all three of these parts together, you will be amazed at the results that you are able to get from the target, and how easy it is to get them to do what you want.

This guidebook is going to spend some time working on the different techniques that you are able to use when it comes to the art of persuasion. This can sometimes be something that we see as a good thing. And often persuasion doesn't have the same evil or bad connotation that manipulation may, even though it is possible that it is going to be used for evil purposes along the way as well.

There is a lot of persuasions that we kind find in the world around us, and it is often going to depend again on the intention that is behind it, and how much choice the other person has. If they are able to see it working and then walk away without feeling any guilt or anything else in the process, then this is seen as a good form of persuasion that still lets you have some kind of choice. But if the manipulator, or the person behind the persuasion, is able to get you to behave in a certain way because it is really hard to walk away and say no, then this is often seen as a bad thing.

Think of some times when you have seen persuasion at work, and it didn't seem like such a bad thing to work with at all. You may have seen countless advertisements out there telling us to purchase this one product, and not another one. We may have had a parent or another family member try to convince us to do something because they needed help or because they thought that it was in our best interests.

We are able to see these kinds of manipulation and find that they are not so bad. We are able to walk away from the advertisements on TV because we have seen a lot of them in our lives, and they all say the same thing over and over again. We know that when a family member, for the most part, tells us about a plan and how they want us to try something, we recognize that it is usually for something that is good for us and we are willing to consider doing something.

But then there are times when the manipulation may not be the best thing for us at all. We find that this persuasion is going to be used against us and that the answer and the reaction to it are not going to be able to benefit us really at all in the process. This is the type of persuasion that we need to be really careful about, the kind that can sometimes sneak up on us without us even knowing. And then we are going to end up losing our control and giving it to the person who is trying to manipulate us.

Staying secret when you manipulate

While we just talked a bit about the three steps or stages to influence, we also need to take a look at what can be known as the final part of this process. It is not really a step like the others but it is important to consider when you do manipulation. When you are working with this process, it is important for you to remember that your intentions need to be kept hidden as much as possible in order to see the results.

Think of it this way. How would you feel if you found out someone was trying to manipulate you against your will? It's likely that you would not feel the best, and would want to stay as far away from them as possible. If someone else finds out that you were working to manipulate them, there are going to be two different things that could show up.

First, it is likely that your target is going to stop trusting you. They will wonder how many other things you have lied about over time and will try to distance themselves from you as much as possible. This is basically going to take away any kind of chance you have to manipulate them now or in the future.

The second issue that you are going to have is when the target sees that you are manipulating, it is going to shed some more light on what you were trying to do. This means that even if you were to try a new kind of tactic for persuasion or manipulation in the future, it is likely they are going to notice it. This is because they no longer trust you, and they are going to start putting all the actions that you do under a microscope to see what adds up and what doesn't.

This means that if you want to be as successful as possible with the process of manipulation, you have to be good at staying secretive about your intentions throughout the whole process. To do this, you need to take things slowly and make sure that you are picking out the right kind of target to work on for all of your needs.

Manipulation is a practice that you can technically use on anyone. There is not going to be any kind of limitation or restriction on who is able to use these techniques, or even when they are able to use them. Of course, most people will also make sure that they are not using the techniques of manipulation when it is seen as something illegal or when it is considered morally wrong. For example, most of the time it is frowned upon to manipulate another person into a relationship with you when it is against their will.

However, these strategies are going to be great to use in situations like negotiations with business because it helps you to make sure that you are getting what you want, helps you to change up the perception that the other person has of you, and other similar manners. There are some people who will use these techniques in the wrong manner and will use the techniques to get what they want, whether it is seen as illegal and unethical or not.

It is so important that if we want to be able to see some success with persuasion or manipulation or anything else that we are doing, that we are able to remain secretive, at least a little bit. We may be able to get away with the analysis and not being as tricky and sneaky as the others because people are always analyzing each other in our modern world. But if you don't be careful with the way that you are using the techniques that come with manipulation and persuasion, then the other person is going to catch on, and you are going to end up in a world of trouble then.

If you are worried about giving yourself away, or if you have had a few close calls that could have derailed the whole thing, this means that you are going through the process too fast. It is much better to take things slow and work through them, forming a good connection with the other person and really getting them to feel like they know you and trust you, rather than just jumping in and hoping that it is all going to work out.

The moment that the other person, the moment that your target, realizes what you are doing against them, and they find out that you are going to use persuasion and manipulation against them for your own benefit, then they are going to want to have nothing to do with you, they may tell others, and you are going to be exposed for all that you are trying to do against them.

It is much better to take your time, do a good analysis, and then pick the technique that you want to use and get them on your side ahead of time. it may take a bit longer, but you will find that this method is much more effective in the long run.

Chapter 11: Techniques And Exercises For Self- Love, Protection (Healthy Boundaries) And Staying Centered & Aligned

Let's now explore the various tips, techniques, exercises and self-development activities best for empaths.

1. Learning to Laugh!

As an empath, it can be very easy to take life too seriously. Because you are used to feeling appreciated and loved for your wise insights, warm and gentle nature and empathic gifts (once you have grown up and found those who appreciate you), there is a tendency to forget to balance serious, deep and soul-level sharing and connection with *letting go* and "*lightening up*." One of the main reasons you suffer when around people or out of your comfort zone is due to your *oversensitivity*; there really is no need to be so sensitive or self-conscious all the time.

So, to help with this as a handy tip, is simply this: just learn to laugh! Not a weird or strange, mean or spiteful laugh (you may know *we are all one* and have a strong heart, but not everyone does!). But I am referring to a real, sincere and open laugh, a laugh which recognizes your oneness in a situation. Everyone is a reflection of you- we are all mirrors, and sometimes what is truly needed to release trapped emotions and blocked energy is a genuine, deep and real laugh. This can be very helpful in many social situations and help you to take things easy, and not so seriously. Combined with the powerful energy exercises, you should find any feelings of anxiousness, tension or low self-esteem disappear in no time. Literally.

When you laugh, you release trapped energy and *raise* it to conscious light. A lot of what is stored is unconscious or residing in our subconscious; therefore, in terms of being an empath, your lack of boundaries and letting harmful or negative energy in may arise from not being away that you are holding on to thoughts or emotions which are not yours. Laughing *shakes things up,* and subsequently enables you to see and feel your own energy. Learning to laugh consciously can help bring you back into your center and personal alignment, from which real change and transformation can occur.

2. Working with your dreams or the subconscious

Looking to your subconscious- and in particular your dreams- can aid greatly in your ability to develop stronger boundaries and enhanced energy in daily life. As already stated you are a natural dream explorer, whether that be lucid dreaming or exploring the dreamworlds at will (consciously). It is in dreams where you have access to your subconscious and, specifically as an empath, you are better able than most to tune in to some subconscious message or universal symbolism for healing and insight. This can affect you in so many ways and on so many levels. Any issue you may be suffering with such as oversensitivity, self-esteem or confidence issues, boundaries, problems with speaking your truth, and stepping fully into your light can be overcome and healed through allowing and being open to receive the wisdom inherent within your subconscious. You are intelligent as well as intuitive and your cells "know," they are conscious and aware. It is in dreams where a part of you becomes triggered, activating some aspect of yourself which is currently in the dark. This in turn increases your natural power and personal authority, simultaneously strengthening your boundaries.

Other ways to connect to your subconscious include journaling, writing, expressing yourself through art therapy or music, and psychoanalysis or any holistic therapy. Holistic therapy is important for your nature, as being an empath is a *holistic experience*. You are not just three-dimensional!

3. Discernment

One of the best ways to get in touch with your empathic superpowers and live your best life is to develop discernment. Now, as an empath, this may be hard as you are such a giving and selfless soul, yet as you are aware this can leave you depleted and victim to the abuse and will of energy vampires, narcissists, and other toxic personalities. Fundamentally, discernment comes through your intuition and advanced emotional wisdom, however you can only access this by being true to yourself and connecting to your unique spiritual and psychically charged gifts. Being an empath inherently involves a psychic and spiritual element, as empathy is literally feeling other people's emotions and feelings and, in more advanced cases, reading others' minds!.Again, we are all connected on a subtle level and empathic power is on the same wave as this.

There are many ways to develop discernment and hopefully the techniques and exercises shared throughout this article can help you do so. One of the main struggles with being an empath is taking on all that is not yours. Thoughts, emotions, wounds, feelings, and impressions all become absorbed through your energy body. This can be highly detrimental to yourself and if left unchecked can lead to repetitive cycles, low moods, and states of suffering. It is natural as an empath to want to heal and help others- it is simply your nature. Yet when taken to extremes this desire to help others ultimately creates a paradox in which you find yourself suffering from no energy and physically, mentally, emotionally, and spiritually feeling drained. This is especially true with narcissists and energy vampires. To counter this, therefore, and to bring some much needed surviving and thriving energy back into your life, there are specific exercises, techniques, and activities you can engage in daily to re-*energize* and re-*center*.

We cover some of these in detail so for now, let's look at these at face value:

Nature. Connecting to nature can aid greatly in your ability to re-energize and recharge yourself. Nature therapy is a powerful way to strengthen your *inner chi*, the life force energy responsible for health, longevity and vitality, and further make your sense of self strong. When your sense of self is strong so are your personal boundaries.

Chakras. Learning about your chakras and becoming knowledgeable of the inner energies at play will allow you to heal yourself on all levels, and also be aware of what may be going on behind the scenes.

We are more than physical bodies- we have subtle bodies and mental, emotional, spiritual and psychic/ astral layers, or planes & dimensions of being. Chakra healing is a sure step to embodying the empath blueprint in its many expressions.

Aura Strengthening and Protecting Exercises. Engaging in exercises that can strengthen and protect your aura can really help you to not only survive, but thrive, in your empathic gifts and in your life holistically.

Meditation and Mindfulness. Incorporating meditation and mindfulness into a daily routine will allow you to develop stronger inner boundaries, a stronger sense of intuition, and more confidence and self-esteem. They will also increase your unique empathic gifts and enhance spiritual awareness, which is intrinsically tied to empathic mindfulness or empathy.

Sound and Mantras: Introducing sound therapy or healing and mantras can re-shape, re-structure and rewire the neurons in your brain to deal with any potential struggles that come with being an empath, while simultaneously allowing for new ways of thinking and perceiving; and further enhancing any psychic or spiritual gifts. Sound therapy is particularly effective for an empathic nature as empaths rely strongly on emotions to be their guide. Emotions are a force.

Psychology and 'the Self:' Exploring psychology and the Self, enable you to learn about the shadow or "dark side" of being an empath so you can bring shadow aspects of yourself to light. Ignorance can be bliss, but allowing other people's thoughts, emotions and subtle energies to influence you (remember- often unconsciously) can be so detrimental and harmful. Knowing yourself and developing awareness with boundaries through wisdom and a strong mind will equally allow for boundaries in all essential areas of your life.

Journaling and Dream Diary: Journaling and beginning a dream diary will allow you to keep a record of your emotions, memories, experiences, and learnings to enable you to *thrive* as an empath. A Dream diary or journal can have a profound effect on waking life through the subconscious messages, symbols, and teachings shown in dreams.

Next we explore:-
Self-love
The healing power of special gemstones and crystals
Meditation
The power of chi and chi balls
Psychic Awareness
Aura Protection
Grounding/ tree meditation
Self-hypnosis

Other extremely important and powerful techniques for developing and integrating the empath blueprint include: Visualization, colors/ color therapy, nature and the elements/ nature therapy and elemental energy, yin and yang, psychic strengthening, hands-on healing/energy healing, and chakra and self- healing.

Aura Protection

One of the most powerful and loving things you could do for yourself is to protect your aura. To some, these techniques may seem slightly "woo," but spirituality and metaphysics are a fundamental part of life. Furthermore, as an empath you naturally resonate with them. Many of the people who are living their dream lives, healthy, abundant, and happy with a strong inner focus, protection and genuine love for life are those who are in tune with their spirituality. Aura protection exercises, therefore, will steer you effectively on the journey to healing and wholeness- and overcoming any sabotaging or destructive thoughts or behaviors.

Working with Crystals. Crystals embody certain energetic frequencies which can interact with our energy fields for a desired effect. Crystals, therefore, are extremely powerful when wishing to strengthen your aura, protect yourself and develop healthy boundaries. The electromagnetic energy field of the crystal or special gemstone interacts with own, healing us and bringing transformation on the subtle planes of existence. Just as colors and the elements have a certain healing effect, and the planets each have their own unique symbolism, so do crystals. Let's look at three main crystals which can help you in everyday life.

Black Tourmaline: Black tourmaline is specifically referred to as a stone of protection. It is grounding, provides a sense of security and trust, and shields you from any "dark," harmful, or negative energy. Connecting to this stone can help you feel stronger inside and increase a sense of confidence, self- esteem and self-empowerment. Meditating with, connecting to, and simply wearing a black tourmaline bracelet, pendant, or necklace will literally shield you from unwanted energies and interactions. _Interesting fact_: quartz crystals are used to power watches!

<u>Amethyst:</u> Amethyst is particularly effective in protecting your aura as it increases your sense of intuition and _inner knowing_. Amethyst is purple and has a majestic feel. It, therefore, can enhance your perception, connect you to your higher mind and inner knowing, and aid in mental clarity in strength when dealing with unsavory characters or situations. Amethyst can act as a psychic shield against negative or harmful energy, therefore, protecting yourself. Again, this crystal can be worn as jewelry or carried around as an individual stone.

Hematite: Hematite is another grounding stone as is helps absorb negative energy and protect your energy field. It can enhance confidence, increase your ability to transform negative situations into positive ones and can calm the mind when responding to stress, anxiety, or worry. Hematite also has an effect on the physical body by its electromagnetic effect on the cells. It can aid in detoxification and strengthen the liver and blood, therefore, enabling you to better protect yourself. Hematite can be carried around and held and connected to for protection and strength in destructive situations.

Self-hypnosis. Self-hypnosis is similar to working with crystals in that your magnetic energy field is strengthened and protected; however, with self-hypnosis, it is your mind having a direct effect as opposed to crystals. You can literally rewire and restructure your mind (through neurological activity, belief, and thought patterns and reconditioning) which can

175

then act as a tool to shield you from harmful energy. Everything can be seen to start in the mind as the mind is the root of all problems, concerns, solutions, and manifestations of recovery.

Self-hypnosis can be performed through many means such as mental reprogramming, mantras, meditation, focused mindfulness, sound therapy, binaural beats and music, reiki and energy healing, and making a conscious effort daily to realign your thoughts and inner focus. You can also see a professional hypnotherapist and gain insights and directions through someone experienced in their field. The key is to remember the power of your mind and to be aware of any unconscious or subconscious beliefs that may be limiting your perspective and holding you down. Once these perspectives are released, your ability to protect yourself through the mind, intention, and thought alone will become clear and amplified. You can also amplify your empathic gifts through the connection self-hypnosis brings to the subconscious.

Connect with nature. Connecting with nature is possibly one of the most effective ways to protect yourself and strengthen your inner boundaries. Nature connects us to all that is, expands our minds, brings mental focus and clarity, heals emotions, releases wounds and traumas, increases our sense of self and therefore confidence, and generally leads to an enhanced and improved way of being. Developing a special relationship with the elements can really help in your ability to remain strong and centered within and to put up better boundaries.

Try the tree meditation below to help center and ground yourself. You will find that your power to protect yourself in harmful situations and ground your sensitivities will be amplified- immensely!

Tree Meditation for Inner Grounding

Visit your favorite nature spot, or a local park, nature reserve or field. Find somewhere quiet or somewhere you feel comfortable. Find a tree with strong roots and a big trunk and sit down with your back straight, gently resting against the trunk, and your knees bent with your feet on the ground. It is best to perform this barefoot as being barefoot grounds your energy with the earth. (Think of chi and life force!)

Close your eyes and focus on your breath. Take note of all the sensations around you, the sounds, smells (hopefully of nature), physical sensations and your connection to this strong and ancient tree. Bring your awareness within while still remaining conscious of your surroundings. Once you are calm, peaceful and centered within with an acute awareness of both your physical body and surroundings, try this.

As you breathe in, visualize a white or golden light being equated with your breath. Watch it travel up your body from your feet to the top of your head and back down again. Do this for 8-10 deep breaths until you feel it starts to come naturally.

Next, visualize that same white or golden light traveling up the trunk of the tree, from its roots all the way up to the top of its leaves- and back down again. Visualize this happening to the tree as you breathe.

Finally, synchronize your breath, the visualization of energy traveling through and up yourself and back down again, and the visualization of energy traveling up the tree from the roots to leaves and back down into the earth into one. Merge the individual parts into *synergy* and feel the energy flow through both you and the tree as one.

This exercise is very powerful for grounding yourself, gaining inner strength and chi and protecting your energy. The effects can be used in a number of circumstances and specifically, will aid in how you respond to and interact with toxic people, use your empathic and intuitive gifts, and regain your confidence psychologically and spiritually. It will, of course, help to strengthen your boundaries.

Crystal Meditation/Connecting to Special Gemstones

Crystals have been used by ancient cultures for thousands of years. As a crystal is formed directly from the earth with thousands of years of celestial energy and planetary projections, each gemstone embodies a certain frequency and vibrational quality. We can, therefore, connect and tune in to crystals to receive their healing power.

As this exercise is intended to connect to crystals for *aura-strengthening and protecting* purposes, here are the main crystals I would recommend purchasing:

Amethyst: Reminder: Amethyst is particularly powerful for your third eye, the brow chakra which relates to all psychic phenomena, extra-sensory perception and awareness, dream states, and enhanced intuition. It helps with protection as it expands awareness, increasing your ability to sense energy and enhances your mental powers of auric-field protection and inner-chi strength.

Quartz: This gem embodies "white light," the purest frequency and a blank canvas for your intentions. This crystal can be programmed with any intention and element to develop the desired effect. If you wish for strength, you can program the crystal with strength. If you need more mental clarity and confidence in speaking your truth or putting up better boundaries, this can be achieved. Any empathic quality or unique ability which corresponds can be amplified. Quartz crystal is a clear canvas.

Black Tourmaline: Reminder: this crystal is specifically known as the protecting and aura-strengthening stone. It embodies a grounding and stabilizing energy and is particularly effective as it encompasses you in a psychic shield which can be integrated into daily life. Black tourmaline raises your vibration and can act as a sponge against dark, harmful, or detrimental energies.

The Meditation:

First, it is essential to cleanse and charge your crystal(s). This is because crystals absorb the energies of others, so cleansing it in water and recharging it in direct sunlight are the best ways to see results.

Create a sacred space, such as with incense, burning oils, frankincense or sage, and either peaceful meditation music, nature sounds, or binaural beats. Get comfortable and hold the crystal in the palm of your left hand with your right hand hovering over the top. Begin your breathing and go within, feeling both your own energy and the crystal's.

Feel into this space for a while and focus your intention on enhancing, expanding, and filling this special gem with light and the frequency you wish to embody. Essentially, fill the crystal up with the quality. Once you have begun to feel a swirl of chi (universal life force energy), you can expand your intentions.

The key with this exercise is to focus on your intention; what exactly you wish to charge the crystal with, your breath and inner state, and the harmonious and synergistic relationship between your own energy field and the crystal's. With practice, it will be very easy to connect to the gemstone's energy field and tune in effortlessly for healing, wholeness and integration, and protection. Remember, it is essential that your crystals are cleansed and recharged.

You can also carry black tourmaline around with you as it is the psychic-shield and energy-field protecting stone. The same applies for Amethyst if you wish to stay connected to your intuitive and psychic powers.

Creating a Chi Ball

Creating a chi ball can be used in any situation, at any time. It is essentially using your mental powers and focused intention to expand and develop the natural chi within and around, and grounding it into an energy ball. This ball of chi can then be used to recharge and re-energize any aspect of yourself. Chi, as you may be aware, is the universal life force which flows through every living thing. It is responsible for your intuitive insight, advanced empathy and emotional intelligence, spirituality, and vitality-longevity- health. Empaths are naturally in tune with the universal life force because we have an advanced emotional and spiritual awareness and capacity.

How to use your chi ball... say you are starting to feel fear or nervous tension in a situation due to your empathic sensitivity, you can take a few minutes to close your eyes, become at peace with yourself and "charge up" an energy ball, and then place it over your heart or stomach (your lower stomach is your sacral chakra, which is often where tricky, painful, or fear-based emotions arise).

If you ever start to lack insight, you can create a chi ball for your intuition and third eye chakra... If you are starting to question yourself, experience old patterns of low self-esteem or confidence issues through absorbing too much information, the chi ball can be created for your heart chakra.... The key is to know that this ball of energy can be created at any time or in any place as the universal life-force energy is always available.

To create your chi ball, visualize a beautiful golden light growing inside your palm chakras. Synchronize your breathing, focus your intention, and really feel this ball of divine energy growing and expanding for your benefit. It is a very effective exercise to incorporate into daily life and can be used to enhance empathy, sight, intuition and any imaginative, creative and intellectual gifts.

A short exercise for self-love

As you must be aware by now, self- love as a sensitive, compassionate and emotionally charged empath is essential.

Frequently engaging in self- care and self-love, therefore is highly beneficial and almost essential to your survival. (On a mental, emotional and spiritual level, at the very least!) Below is a very simple yet highly effective exercise for increasing self-love. As explored, self- love is one of the main steps to healing psychology and spiritually, and protecting your boundaries. First, purchase a rose quartz crystal gemstone. Rose quartz specifically relates to *the heart* and has vibrational qualities of enhancing unconditional love, compassion, kindness, empathy, and forgiveness. Rose quartz is essentially known as the heart chakra stone.

Cleanse and charge your crystal. Firstly, cleanse your crystal in cold running water and then charge it in direct sunlight. Crystals respond to the natural elements and also pick up and store energy, therefore, it is essential that you cleanse and charge your crystal of any lingering energies.

Create a sacred space either outside in a favorite nature spot, or inside where you feel comfortable.

Hold the rose quartz in the palm of your left hand with your right hand hovering over the top. Similar to the visualization expressed earlier, visualize a beautiful, warm and loving glowing light emanating from both the crystal and your right hand. Practice your breathing.

Make sure your breath is deep, calm, and steady with a slightly euphoric feeling or at least a deep sense of enhanced awareness. Breathe deeply within and into the crystal, still picturing a glowing light growing. Once you feel calm and centered with a steady glow in between your hands and any tingling or energetic sensations, set your intention. Focus your mental power on love, healing, forgiveness, and positive energy filling up the rose quartz. Project these intentions while similarly visualizing and feeling the glowing light.

Sit with this experience for a while and pour your love and positive energy into the crystal. Once you feel ready, let go of all thoughts and intentions and be still. Keep breathing steady, but be still inside your mind; allowing your energy to merge with the crystals. Feel yourself receiving the rose quartz's beautiful healing vibrations of love and forgiveness and feel its subtle pulse interacting with yours.

This short but powerful exercise can be done anywhere and anytime once you have established a connection. You can also purchase rose quartz earrings, pendant or smaller crystal to keep in your pocket or purse and carry around with you. Always remember the *intention* and inner qualities of rose quartz and allow yourself to receive love on a daily basis.

The science of crystals: Gemstones have been used for thousands of years due to the knowledge of their healing power. They have metaphysical properties which allow them to be catalysts for healing and wholeness to occur. Nowadays we use quartz crystals to power watches yet ancient cultures were also aware of the inner power of crystals. Essentially, the electromagnetic energy field of the crystal or gemstone interacts without the electromagnetic energy field, affecting the mind, emotions, body, and spirit in addition to enhancing the qualities associated with the specific crystal.

Psychic Awareness exercises

As all of our bodies are connected, increasing your psychic awareness and intuition can lead to enhanced perception, insight, and connection to a higher power. This, in turn, helps you connect to your true empathic nature and embrace the qualities which make you who you are. Your heart (where empathy arises) and higher mind (where your spiritual awareness comes forth) are intrinsically linked.

The crystal exercises can be used to increase your psychic and spiritual awareness, therefore allowing yourself to thrive as an empath. Spiritual healing, shamanic healing, sound therapy, working with the elements, self- healing and learning a Healing Art are all other ways to enhance your psychic powers and gifts. There is not a greater intuition than the empath intuition...

Chapter 12: Emotional Healing Methods

Now that you have done the work to heal yourself and practice some thorough self-reflection, it may be time to start exploring the different types of healing to which empaths are best suited. This chapter will review healing methods that are likely to work best for emotional empaths, but there is no reason why other empath types should not experiment with these methods if they feel drawn to them.

Meditation
Of all the empathic healing methods available, meditation is perhaps the most

easily accessible for those with limitations, be they financial, logistical, temporal, or otherwise. Anyone can learn to meditate, at any age, in any place, at any time, for as short or long of a session as they can manage.

Meditation requires at least a few minutes of quiet and stillness. It can be practiced standing, sitting, lying down, or in a challenging yoga pose. The goal is to close your eyes, breathe mindfully, and allow yourself to recognize your own thought patterns without being consumed or overpowered by them. It is a common misconception that you can only successfully meditate with a clear mind. It's not about *not* thinking; it's thinking *about* your thoughts, recognizing that they are only thoughts (not reality) and that you have the power to embrace them or to let them go. Some people prefer to use meditation guides—classes or audio recordings that provide ideas or concepts to meditate upon. Others find it more productive to simply let their mind wander and ride the wave of thoughts, while still staying healthily detached from them. This would allow you to encounter a thought that causes you anxiety—say, for instance, that in the midst of a meditation session, you suddenly remember an overdue bill that you've forgotten to pay—but rather than spinning into a panic or buying into negative beliefs about yourself, your detached mind might instead think: "I wonder why this thought came up at this particular moment. Normally, I'd fly into a panic over this. What other reactions could I choose that might serve me better?"

Though meditation can be simplified into a mental exercise so simple, even kindergartners can grasp it, there is also no end to the potential depth and complexity of this healing art. Incorporating just a few minutes of meditation into your routine on a weekly or daily basis can work to enhance mental and emotional clarity, to replenish energy and focus, and to manage stress. By contrast, doing intense meditative work, whether guided or alone, for extended periods of time—an hour each day, or even multiple hours—can have an extraordinary transformative impact on every aspect of your life, from your physical health to your mental acuity and productivity levels.

Even if you only have time to practice for five minutes a day, meditation is one of the most effective ways to put yourself back in the mental and emotional driver's seat of your own life. When we are overwhelmed by fast-paced schedules, technological acceleration, busy social and familial networks, and constant financial pressures, it can be easy to feel like our lives are happening to us, whether we like it or not. By taking a few minutes to pause and re-center ourselves, we are better able to refocus our energies on the things that matter most; to extract the negative thoughts and feelings that are not ours to carry and are not serving us, and to remember that our lives are mostly what we make of them.

Meditation practices can be extremely productive, sometimes leading to epiphanies, mental breakthroughs, and emotional fulfillment. It isn't always a triumphant experience, though, which is why empaths should feel encouraged to stick to a routine practice for at least a full month before they make any judgments about its value or effectiveness. Sometimes, meditation can lead us through complex emotional experiences, like anger release or trauma resurfacing, both of which can initially lead us to feel temporarily worse before we start to feel better. In the long run, though, meditation is like exercise for the brain and the soul; it strengthens us from the inside out.

Ceremonial Healing

There are many different kinds of ceremonial healing rituals; some are attached to spiritual faiths and derived from ancient traditions, such as Native

American, Wiccan or Pagan healing ceremonies, while other New Age traditions aim to incorporate knowledge from multiple cultures and schools of thought, making rituals accessible to experienced practitioners and novices alike.

Ceremonial healing rituals can also be focused on physical ailments, but here, we'll touch on two of the most popular emotional healing methods. You may find many other ritual services are available to you if you contact lightworkers and healers in your area.

Energy Shields

Creating an energy shield is something you can do for yourself, even with very little experience. It is largely a mental visualization exercise, in which you imagine a shield of energy drawn around yourself, and define very clearly what you want to let inside, what must be kept out, and what type of energy the shield is made of. Energy shields can be protective or deflective; they can be solid and rigid or woven like a grid to allow certain elements in while guarding against others. They may be drawn to help us accomplish our goals, or they may be created to help us ward off toxic, destructive energies.

If you are struggling to make your own energy shield effective, it may be wise to seek out an energy healer to help with a ceremonial shield creation. This may involve a consultation, meditation, crystal healing work, a sonic healing element, and maybe the repetition of mantras or affirmations. Logistics will vary, depending on the healer you choose to work with. Whatever the process, an energy shield created by two empaths will be exponentially stronger and more tangible than any shield created by a lone individual.

In a ceremony like this, it's important to be as honest and transparent as possible with your healer and to stay open-minded. Their rituals may seem odd to you, but at the end of the day, your energy shield will only ever be as strong as your belief in it.